CAKES & CUPCAKES

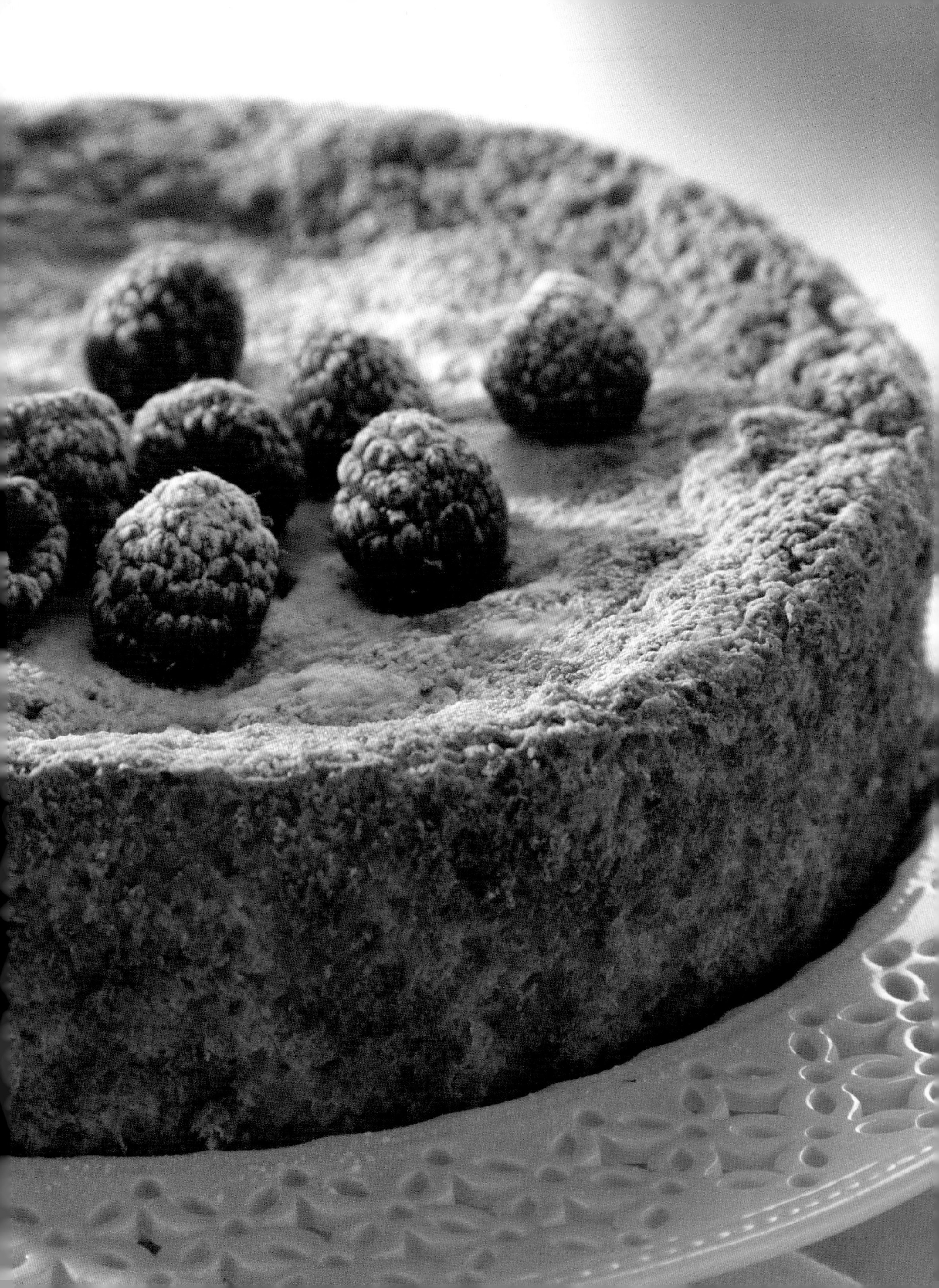

CAKES & CUPCAKES

Great baking ideas, from fancy cupcakes to magnificent muffins

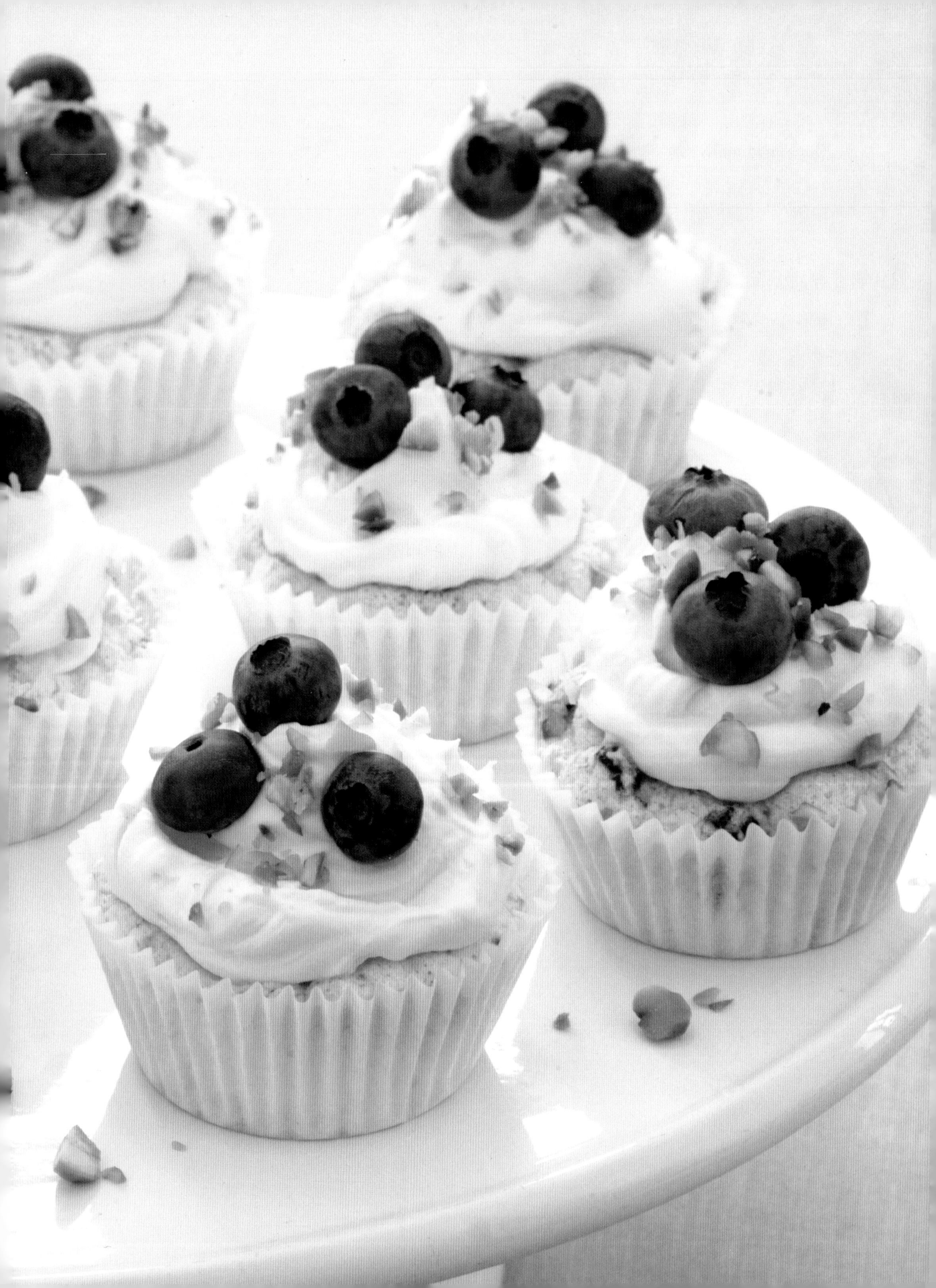

CONTENTS

Guide to symbols

The recipes in this book are accompanied by symbols that alert you to important information.

 Tells you how many people the recipe serves, or how much is produced.

 Indicates how much time you will need to prepare and cook a dish. Next to this symbol you will also find out if additional time is required for such things as marinating, standing, proving, or cooling. You need to read the recipe to find out exactly how much extra time is needed.

 Alerts you to what has to be done before you can begin to cook the recipe, or to parts of the recipe that take a long time to complete.

 Denotes that special equipment is required. Where possible, alternatives are given.

 Accompanies freezing information.

Techniques

Prepare and line a cake tin

Greasing then flouring or lining your tin ensures that baked layers turn out cleanly and easily.

1 Melt unsalted butter (unless your recipe states otherwise) and use a pastry brush to apply a thin, even layer over the bottom and sides of the tin, making sure to brush butter into the corners.

2 Then, sprinkle a small amount of flour into the tin. Shake the pan so the flour coats the bottom and rotate the tin to coat the sides. Turn the tin upside down and tap to remove the excess flour.

3 Or, to line with greaseproof paper instead of flouring, stand the tin on the paper and draw around the base. Cut out just inside the line.

4 Place the piece of greaseproof paper directly on to the greased bottom of the cake tin. It should fit neatly inside and into the corners of the tin.

Make sponge cake

This method will produce feather-light sponge. Use 2 x 20cm (8in) sandwich tins to make 2 sponges, which you can fill with fruit or cream if you like.

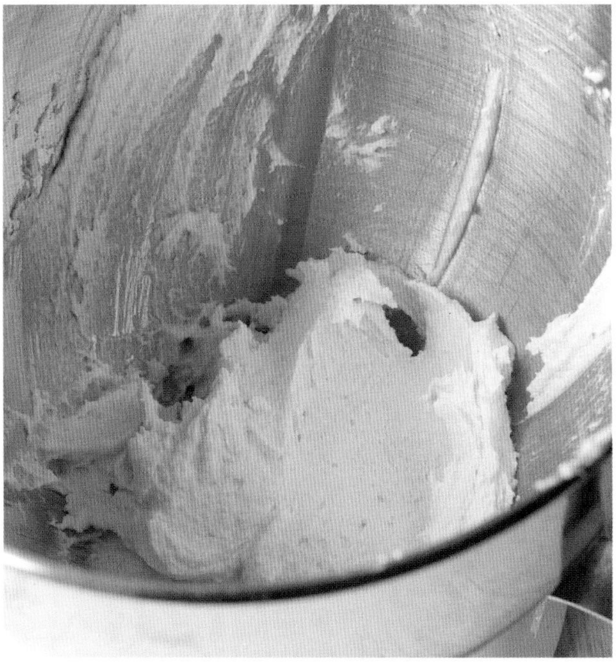

1 Preheat the oven to 180°C (350°F/Gas 4). In a bowl, cream together 225g (8 oz) softened butter and 225g (8 oz) caster sugar with an electric mixer or wooden spoon until pale and fluffy.

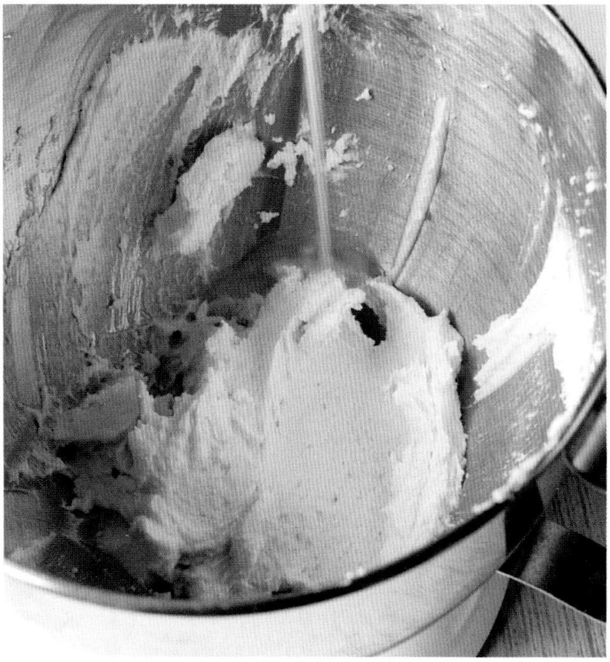

2 Lightly beat 4 room-temperature eggs. Add them little by little to the butter and sugar, beating well. Add a tablespoon of sifted flour, taken from 225g (8 oz) self-raising flour, to prevent it from curdling.

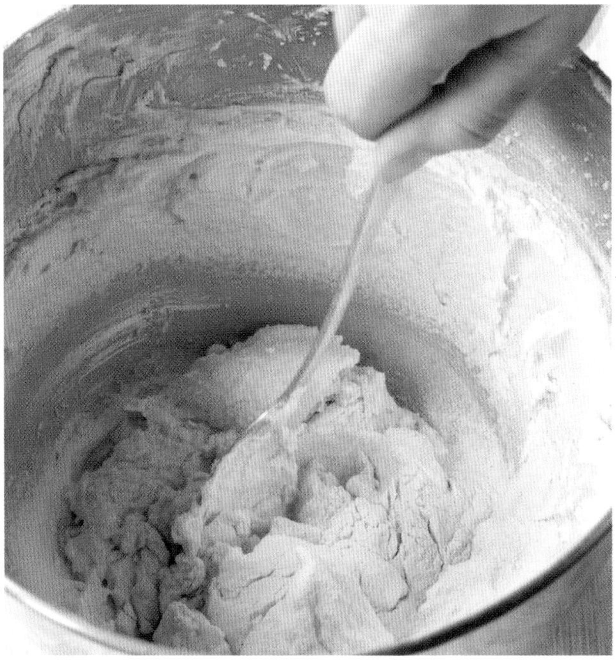

3 Once all the egg is added, use a spoon to fold in the rest of the flour. The mixture should drop off the spoon easily when it is ready. Add a tablespoon of water if the mixture is too thick.

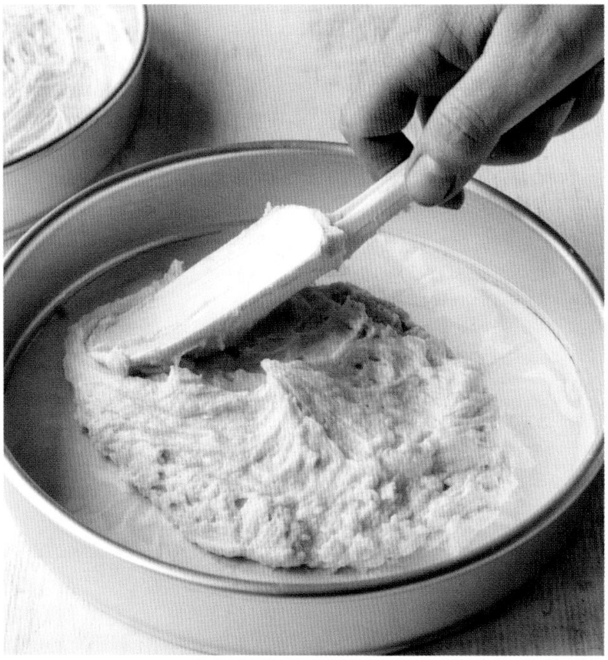

4 Divide the mixture between 2 tins, and smooth out. Bake for 20 minutes, or until the cakes have risen, are golden, and feel springy to the touch. Allow to cool slightly in the tins before turning out.

Vanilla cupcakes

Coloured buttercream icing and small decorations transform these simple cupcakes into firm family favourites.

INGREDIENTS

225g (8 oz) unsalted butter, softened
225g (8 oz) caster sugar
225g (8 oz) self-raising flour
1 tsp baking powder
4 eggs
1 tsp pure vanilla extract
buttercream icing (see p92), coloured
  pale pink and yellow
pink metallic balls, to decorate
  (optional)

METHOD

1 Preheat the oven to 180°C (350°F/Gas 4). Line a bun tray with 18–20 paper baking cases.
2 Place the butter, sugar, flour, baking powder, eggs, and vanilla extract in a large mixing bowl and beat with an electric whisk for 2–3 minutes, or until well combined. Spoon into the paper baking cases and bake for 18 minutes, or until risen and golden brown. Transfer to a wire rack to cool completely.
3 Fill the piping bag with either pink or yellow icing. Pipe a swirl of on top of each cupcake and add a few metallic balls.

makes 18–20

prep 15 mins,
plus cooling
• cook 18 mins

bun tray • paper baking
cases • piping bag •
electric whisk

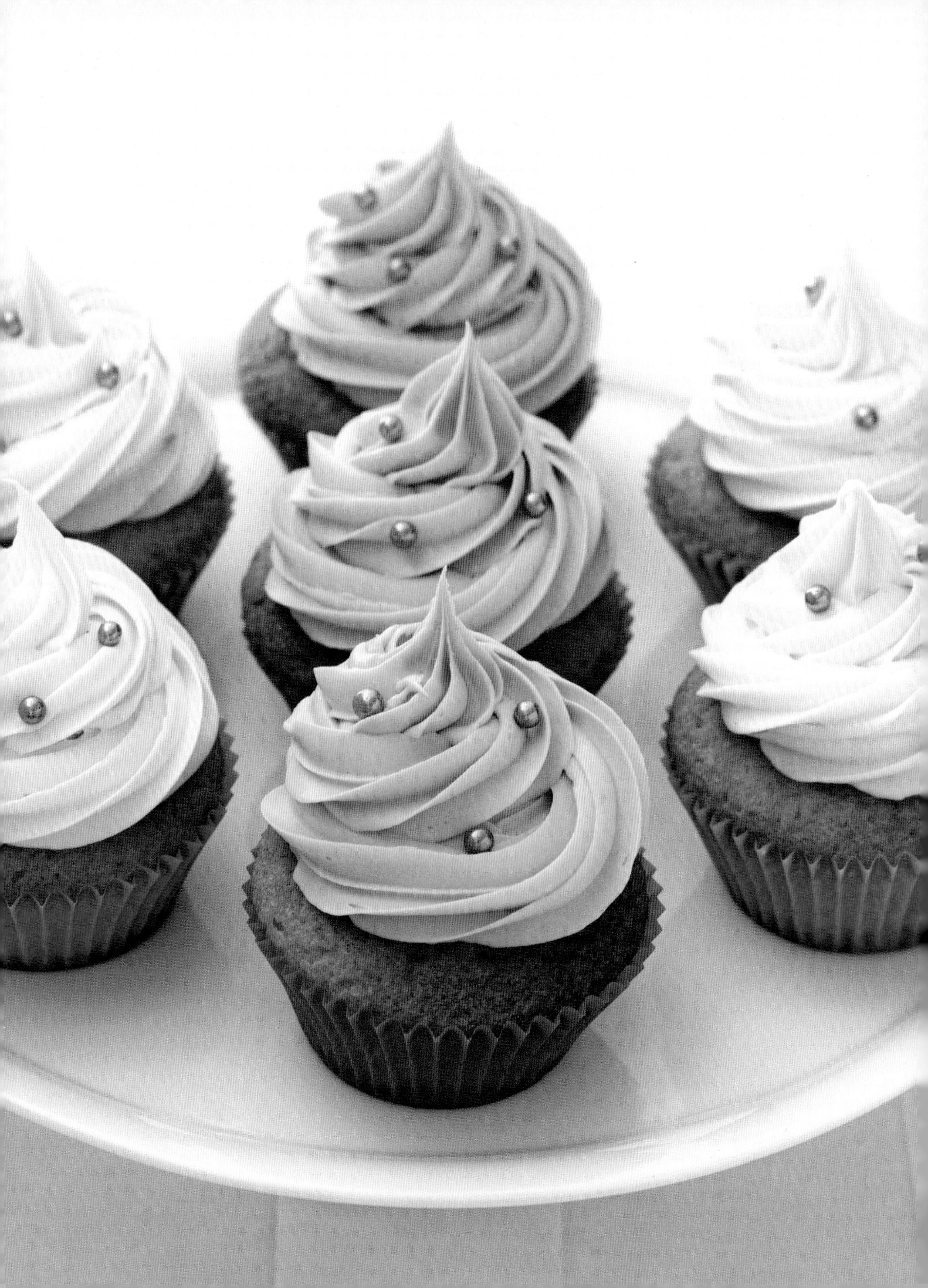

Raspberry cupcakes

Elegant cakes that are perfect with after-dinner coffee.

INGREDIENTS

225g (8 oz) unsalted butter, at room
   temperature
225g (8 oz) caster sugar
225g (8 oz) self-raising flour
1 tsp baking powder
4 eggs
3 tbsp ground almonds
150g (5½ oz) raspberries,
   plus 18–20 extra, to decorate
175g (6 oz) white chocolate,
   plus extra, grated, to decorate

METHOD

1 Preheat the oven to 180°C (350°F/Gas 4). Line a bun tray with 18–20 cupcake cases.
2 Place the butter, caster sugar, flour, baking powder, and eggs in a large mixing bowl
   and beat with a wooden spoon, electric hand whisk, or mixer until well combined.
   Stir in the almonds and raspberries, then spoon the mixture into the paper baking
   cases and bake for 18 minutes, or until risen and golden brown. Place on a wire rack
   to cool completely.
3 Put the white chocolate in a heatproof bowl, and melt it over a pan of barely
   simmering water, stirring occasionally until the chocolate is melted and smooth.
   Drizzle the chocolate over the top of the cupcakes. Decorate each one with grated
   white chocolate, and a raspberry.

makes 18–20

prep 15 mins
• cook 18 mins

standard bun tray
• standard cupcake
cases • piping bag

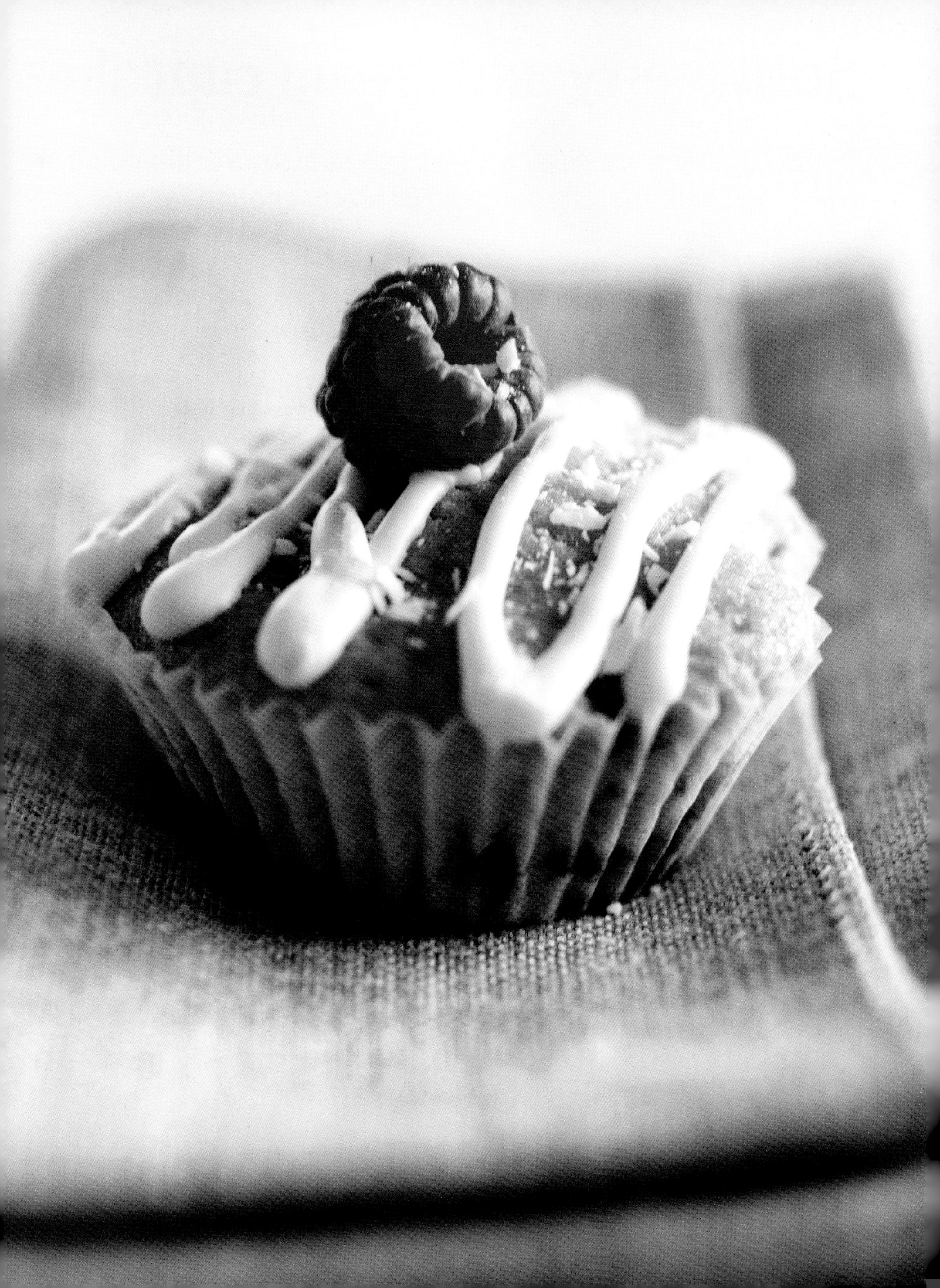

Strawberry and cream cupcakes

These cupcakes are filled with a fresh strawberry filling and are a luscious treat for afternoon tea or pretty enough for a dessert.

INGREDIENTS

2 eggs, separated
115g (4 oz) caster sugar
85g (3 oz) unsalted butter, at room
  temperature
85g (3 oz) self-raising flour
30g (1 oz) cornflour
¼ tsp pure vanilla extract

For the filling and topping

225g (8 oz) strawberries
30g (1 oz) caster sugar
A few drops of lemon juice
150ml (5fl oz) double or whipping cream

METHOD

1 Preheat the oven to 200°C (400°F/Gas 6). Line the bun tray with 12 cupcake cases.

2 Place the egg whites in a clean, dry glass or metal bowl and whisk until stiff, then whisk in 1 tbsp of the sugar and set aside. In another bowl, beat the butter and sugar with a wooden spoon or an electric hand whisk until light and fluffy. Beat in the egg yolks. Sift the flour and cornflour over the surface and beat in with 2 tbsp hot water plus the vanilla extract. Gently fold in the whisked egg whites with a metal spoon. Do not over-mix, but make sure all the egg white is incorporated.

3 Spoon a heaped dessert spoon of the mixture into the cupcake cases, and bake for about 12 minutes, or until well risen, golden, and the centres spring back when lightly pressed. Transfer to a wire rack to cool.

4 Meanwhile, prepare the filling and topping. Select 6 small or 3 large strawberries cut into halves or quarters, including their green hulls, and reserve for decoration. Hull and chop the remainder and sweeten to taste with a little of the sugar, and sharpen with a few drops of lemon juice. Whip the cream and the remaining sugar until peaking.

5 Cut out a circle of sponge from each cake so you end up with a small well in the centre, leaving a 5mm (¼in) border all round. Fill with the chopped strawberries. Pipe or spoon the whipped cream on top, and put a strawberry half, or quarter, on the top of each. Place the cut out rounds of sponge at a jaunty angle to the side of the strawberries and press gently into the cream to secure.

makes 12

prep 15 mins • cook 12 mins

12-cup standard bun tray • standard cupcake cases

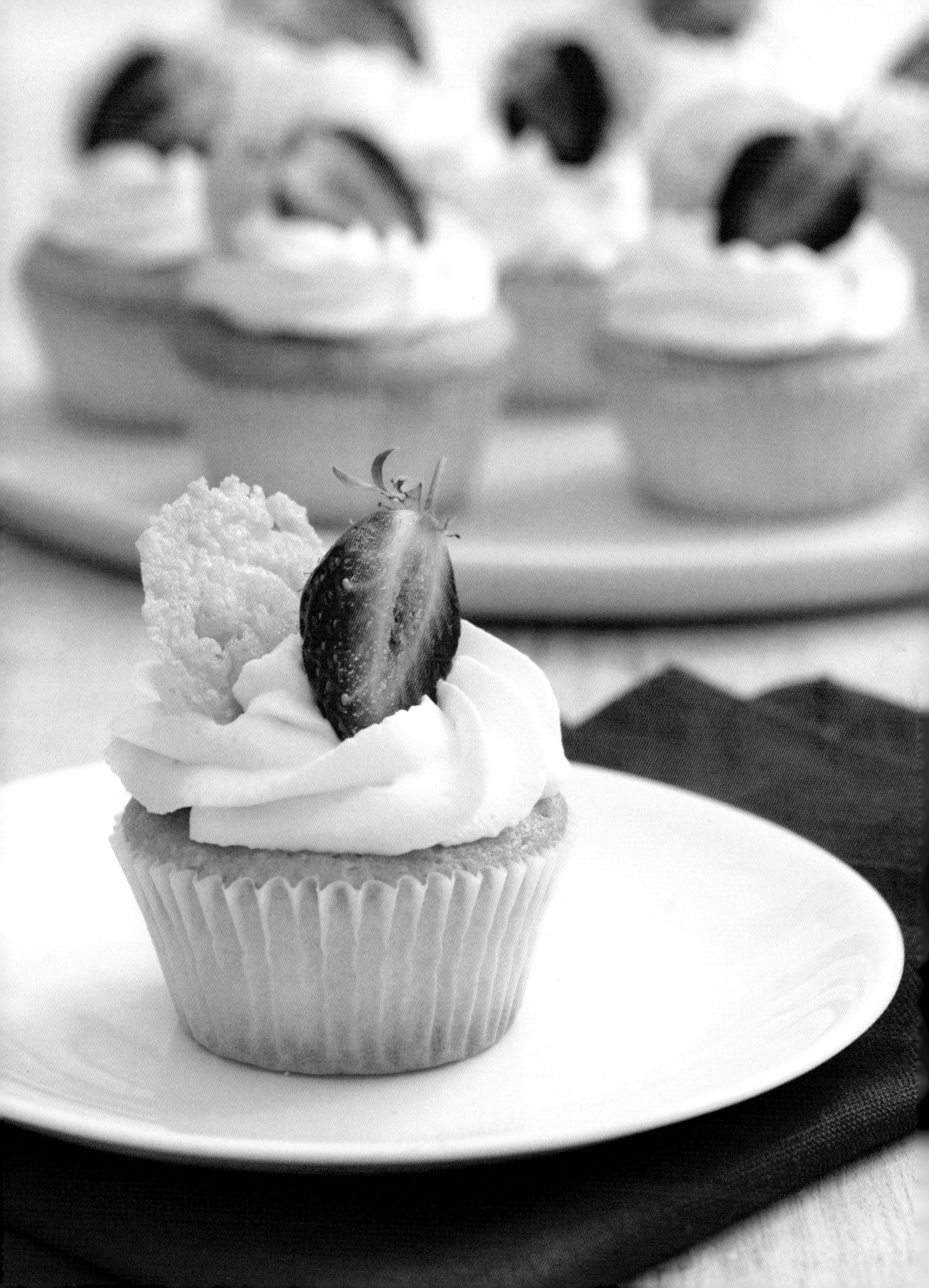

Cherry and coconut cupcakes

This classic combination of flavours is always popular. If you like, the cakes can be coloured pink as well as the icing.

INGREDIENTS

115g (4 oz) glacé cherries, quartered
115g (4 oz) butter, at room temperature
115g (4 oz) caster sugar
2 eggs
85g (3 oz) self-raising flour
55g (2 oz) desiccated coconut, plus extra
   for dusting
1½ tsp baking powder
few drops of natural pink food colouring
   (optional)

For the icing

175g (6 oz) butter, at room temperature
350g (12 oz) icing sugar, sifted
4 tsp milk
few drops of natural pink food colouring
25g (scant 1 oz) desiccated coconut
12 glacé cherries

METHOD

1 Preheat the oven to 180°C (350°F/Gas 4). Line a bun tray with 12–15 cupcake cases. Wash, dry, and quarter the cherries.

2 Put the butter, sugar, eggs, flour, coconut, and baking powder in a large mixing bowl and beat well with a wooden spoon, an electric hand whisk, or mixer until light and fluffy. Add the quartered cherries. If using, add a few drops of pink food colouring and beat briefly again.

3 Spoon the mixture into the cupcake cases, and bake for about 15 minutes, or until well risen, golden, and the centres spring back when lightly pressed. Transfer to a wire rack to cool.

4 To make the icing, beat the softened butter in a bowl. Gradually beat in the icing sugar and milk until soft and fluffy. Beat in a few drops of pink food colouring. Pipe or spoon the icing on top of the cupcakes, and top each with a dusting of desiccated coconut and a glacé cherry.

makes 12–15

prep 15 mins
• cook 15 mins

standard bun
tray • standard
cupcake cases

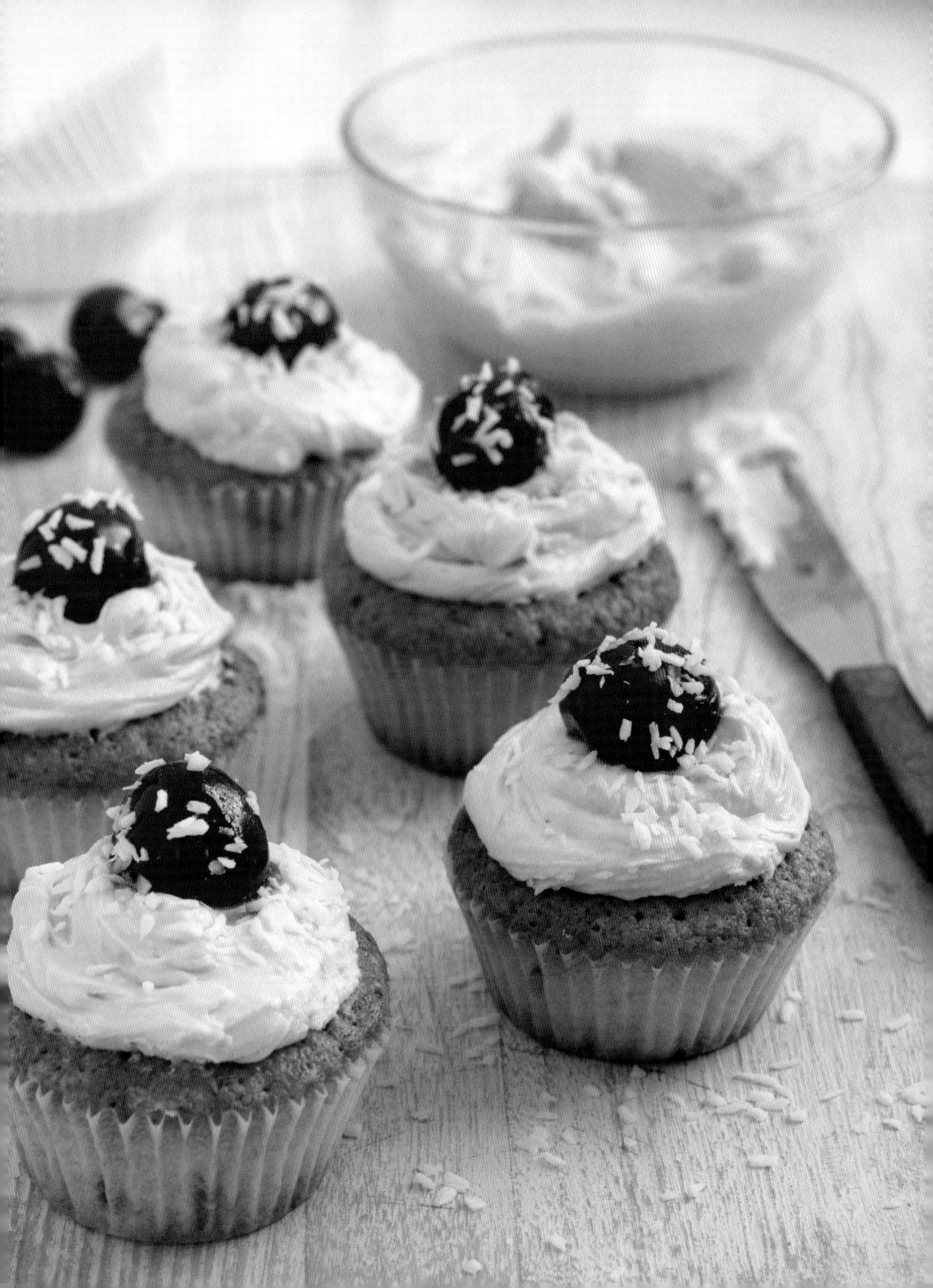

Cinnamon apple and sultana cupcakes

Apples and sultanas are an infallible combination and seem made for each other in these delicious, moist cupcakes.

INGREDIENTS

115g (4 oz) butter, at room temperature
115g (4 oz) caster sugar
2 eggs
115g (4 oz) self-raising flour
½ tsp baking powder
2 tsp ground cinnamon
3 green eating apples, peeled and grated, discarding cores
55g (2 oz) sultanas

For the icing

225g (8 oz) unsalted butter, at room temperature
450g (1 lb) icing sugar, sifted
2 tbsp lemon juice
ground cinnamon, to dust

METHOD

1 Preheat the oven to 180°C (350°F/Gas 4). Line the muffin tray with 12 muffin cases.
2 Put the butter, sugar, eggs, flour, baking powder, and cinnamon in a large mixing bowl and beat well with a wooden spoon, electric hand whisk, or mixer until light and fluffy. Add the grated apples and sultanas and beat briefly again.
3 Spoon the mixture into the muffin cases, and bake for about 15 minutes, or until well risen, golden, and the centres spring back when lightly pressed. Transfer to a wire rack to cool.
4 To make the icing, beat the softened unsalted butter in a bowl. Gradually beat in the icing sugar and lemon juice until soft and fluffy. Pipe or spoon the icing on top of the cupcakes and dust with cinnamon.

 makes 12

 prep 15 mins • cook 15 mins

 12-cup muffin tin • muffin cases

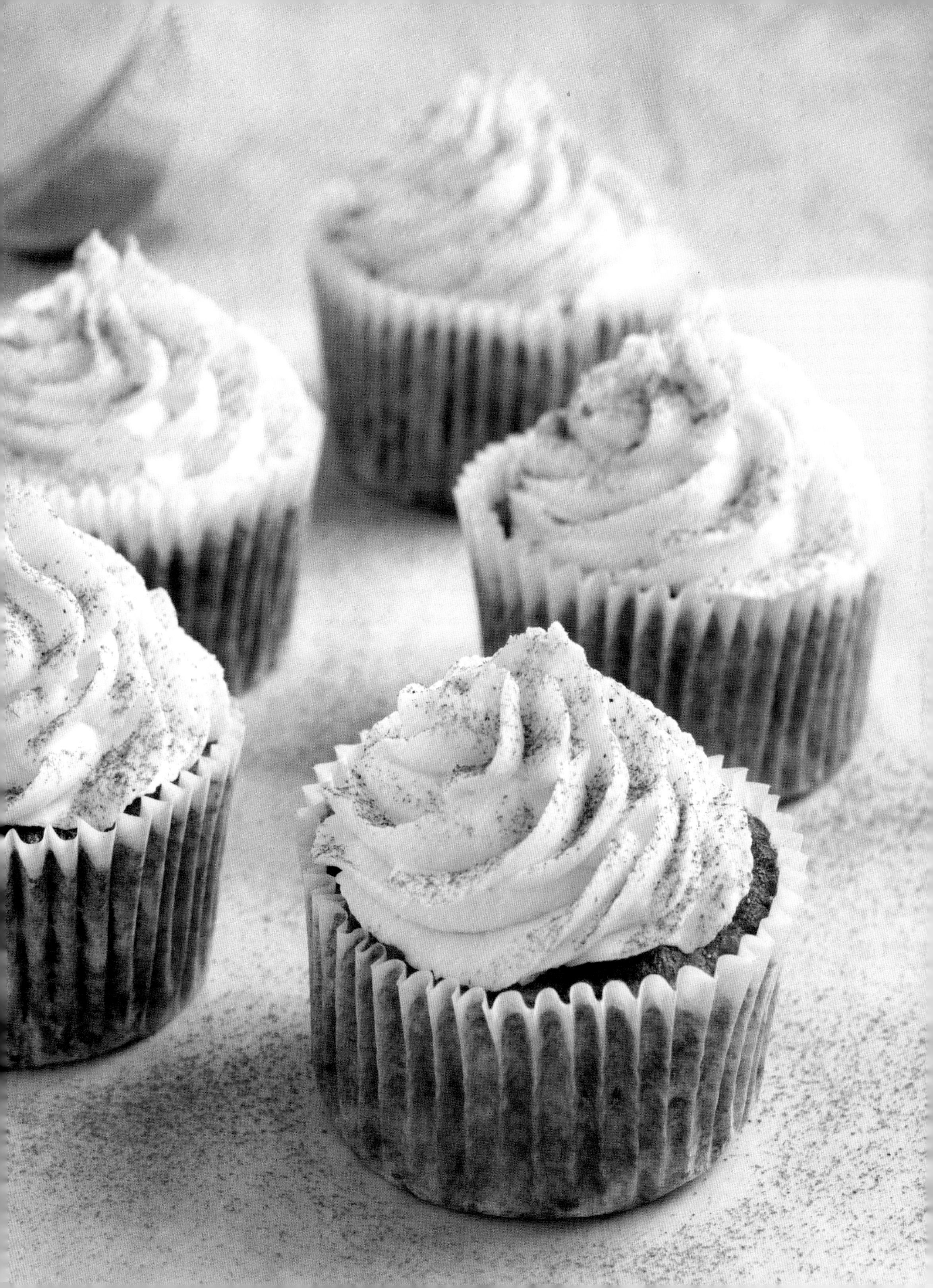

Blueberry and pistachio angel cupcakes

These look beautiful and taste sublime. Serve for tea or dessert.

INGREDIENTS

55g (2 oz) shelled pistachio nuts
2 large egg whites
pinch of salt
½ tsp cream of tartar
115g (4 oz) caster sugar
40g (1¼ oz) plain flour
20g (¾ oz) cornflour
¼ tsp natural almond extract

¼ tsp pure vanilla extract
85g (3 oz) dried blueberries

For the cream cheese frosting

150ml (5fl oz) double cream
4 tbsp icing sugar
140g (5 oz) cream cheese
a few fresh or extra dried blueberries (optional)

METHOD

1 Preheat the oven to 160°C (325°F/Gas 3). Line the bun tray with 12 cupcake cases.

2 Put the pistachios in a bowl, cover with boiling water and leave to stand for 5 minutes. Drain, then rub off the skins in a clean tea towel. Finely chop the nuts. Set aside half for decoration.

3 Place the egg whites in a clean, dry glass or metal bowl and lightly whisk with a balloon whisk or an electric hand whisk until foamy. Whisk in the salt and cream of tartar, and continue to whisk until the egg whites stand in stiff peaks.

4 Sift the sugar, flour, and cornflour over the egg whites, add the almond and vanilla extracts, the dried blueberries, and half the chopped nuts, then fold in gently with a metal spoon until just combined.

5 Spoon the mixture into the cupcake cases, and bake for about 25 minutes, or until risen, pale biscuit-coloured, and just firm to the touch. Transfer to a wire rack to cool.

6 To make the frosting, place the cream in a bowl and lightly whip with the icing sugar. Then whisk in the cream cheese until softly peaking. Spoon the frosting on top of the angel cakes and decorate with the reserved pistachio nuts and a few fresh or dried blueberries, if using.

makes 12

prep 25 mins
• cook 25 mins

12-cup standard
bun tray • standard
cupcake cases

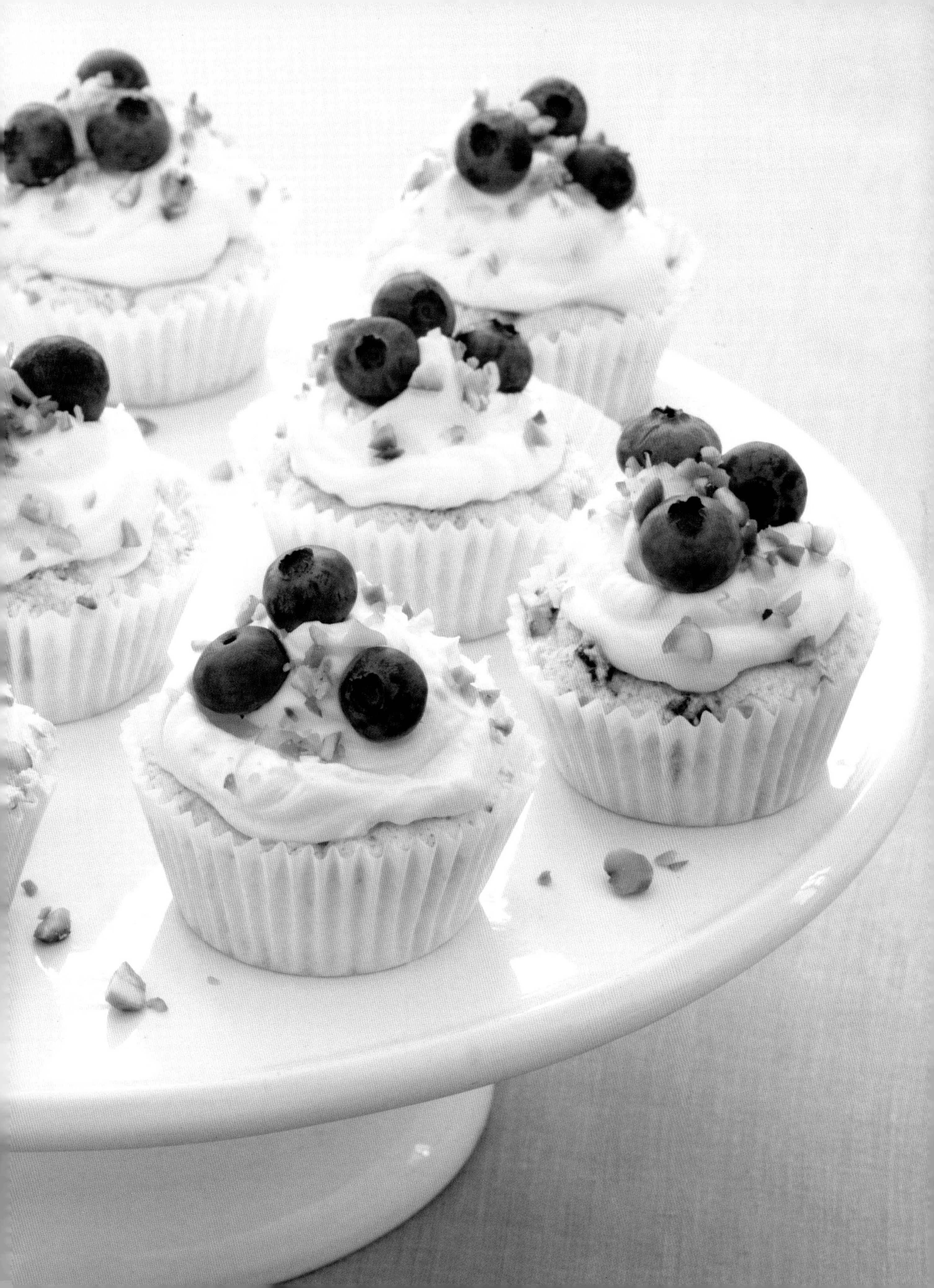

Coffee walnut cupcakes

A stylish cupcake for morning coffee or afternoon tea.

INGREDIENTS

85g (3 oz) walnut halves, finely chopped
115g (4 oz) butter, at room temperature
115g (4 oz) caster sugar
115g (4 oz) self-raising flour
½ tsp baking powder
2 eggs
2 tsp instant coffee granules, dissolved
   in 2 tsp hot water

For the coffee icing

1 tbsp instant coffee granules, dissolved
   in 1 tbsp hot water
175g (6 oz) butter, at room temperature
350g (12 oz) icing sugar, sifted
12 walnut halves

METHOD

1 Preheat the oven to 180°C (350°F/Gas 4). Line a bun tray with 12–15 cupcake cases.

2 Place the butter, caster sugar, flour, baking powder, eggs, and the instant coffee solution in a large mixing bowl and beat well with a wooden spoon, electric hand whisk, or mixer until light and fluffy. Fold in the walnuts with a metal spoon.

3 Spoon the mixture into the cupcake cases, and bake for about 15 minutes, or until well risen, golden, and the centres spring back when lightly pressed. Transfer to a wire rack to cool.

4 Meanwhile, make the icing. Place the instant coffee solution in a bowl. Beat in the butter and gradually add the sifted icing sugar, beating until light and fluffy. Pipe or spoon the icing on top of the cooled cupcakes. Decorate each with a walnut half.

makes 12–15

prep 15 mins
• cook 15 mins

standard bun
tray • standard
cupcake cases

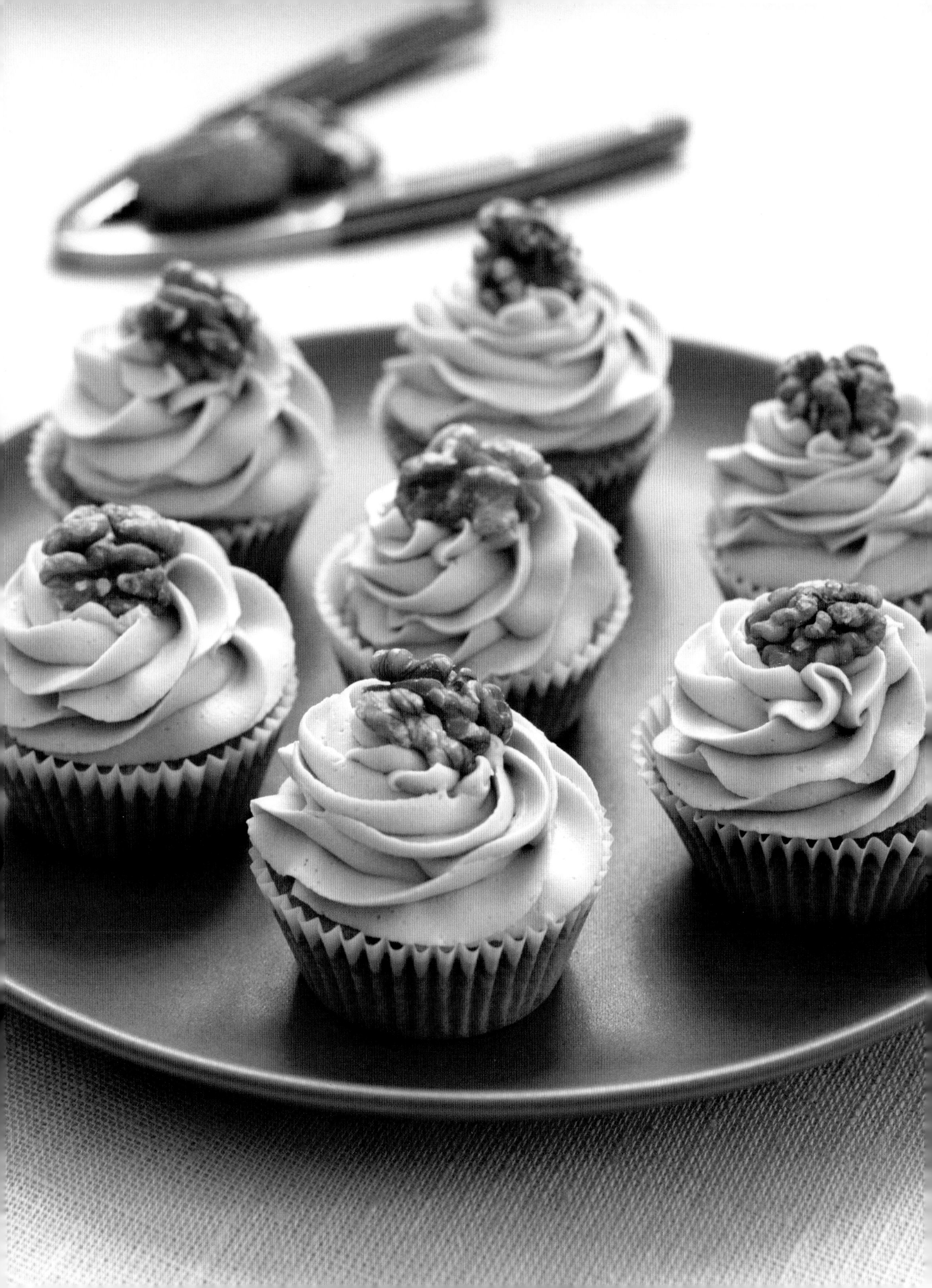

Chocolate-frosted cupcakes

Kids will adore the creamy, chocolatey icing on these dainty cakes.

INGREDIENTS

125g (4½ oz) butter, softened
125g (4½ oz) caster sugar
2 large eggs, beaten
125g (4½ oz) self-raising flour, sifted
1 tsp pure vanilla extract
1 tbsp milk, if necessary

For the icing

100g (3½ oz) icing sugar
15g (½ oz) cocoa powder
100g (3½ oz) butter, softened
few drops of vanilla pure extract
25g (scant 1 oz) milk chocolate
or dark chocolate, shaved with
a vegetable peeler

METHOD

1 Preheat the oven to 190°C (375°F/Gas 5). Line the muffin tin with paper cases. Place the butter and sugar in a bowl, and whisk with an electric hand whisk or mixer until pale and fluffy. Beat in the eggs a little at a time, adding a little of the flour each time. Add the vanilla extract, then the rest of the flour, and mix until smooth and combined – the mixture should drop easily off the beaters. If it doesn't, stir in the milk. Divide the mixture between the paper cases using two teaspoons. Bake for 20 minutes, or until risen, golden, and firm to the touch. Transfer the cupcakes to a wire rack to cool.

2 To make the icing, sift the icing sugar and cocoa powder, into a bowl, add the butter and the vanilla extract, and whisk with an electric hand whisk until the mixture is light and fluffy. Ice the cupcakes, giving the top of each one a swirly design. Scatter over the chocolate shavings.

makes 12

prep 25 mins
• cook 20 mins

12-hole muffin tin
• paper cases
• electric hand
whisk or mixer

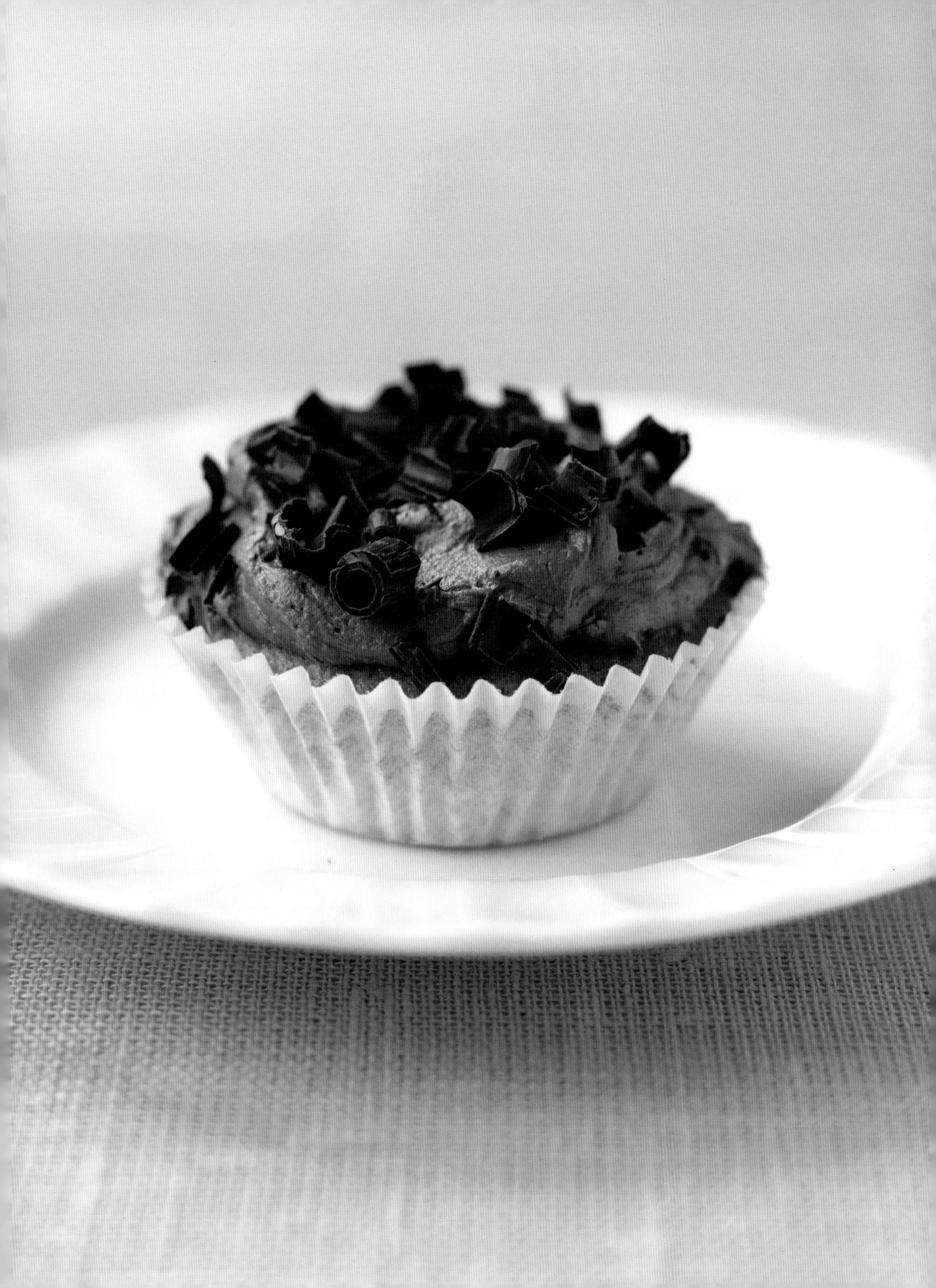

Apple muffins

These are lovely served straight from the oven for breakfast.

INGREDIENTS

1 Golden Delicious apple, peeled and chopped
2 tsp lemon juice
115g (4 oz) light demerara sugar, plus extra for sprinkling
200g (7 oz) plain flour
85g (3 oz) wholemeal flour
4 tsp baking powder

1 tbsp ground mixed spice
½ tsp salt
60g (2 oz) pecan nuts, chopped
250ml (9fl oz) milk
4 tbsp sunflower oil
1 egg, beaten

METHOD

1 Preheat the oven to 200°C (400°F/Gas 6). Line a 12-hole American-style muffin tin with paper cases and set aside. Put the apple in a bowl, add the lemon juice, and toss. Add 4 tablespoons of the sugar and set aside for 5 minutes.

2 Meanwhile, sift the plain and wholemeal flours, baking powder, mixed spice, and salt into a large bowl, tipping in any bran left in the sieve. Stir in the remaining sugar and pecans then make a well in the centre of the dry ingredients.

3 Beat together the milk, oil, and egg, then add the apple. Tip the wet ingredients into the centre of the dry ingredients and mix together lightly to make a lumpy batter.

4 Spoon the mixture into the paper cases, filling each case three-quarters full. Bake the muffins for 20–25 minutes, or until the tops are peaked and brown. Transfer the muffins to a wire rack and sprinkle with extra sugar. Eat warm or cooled.

makes 12

prep 10 mins
• cook 20–25 mins

12-hole American-style muffin tin
• paper cases

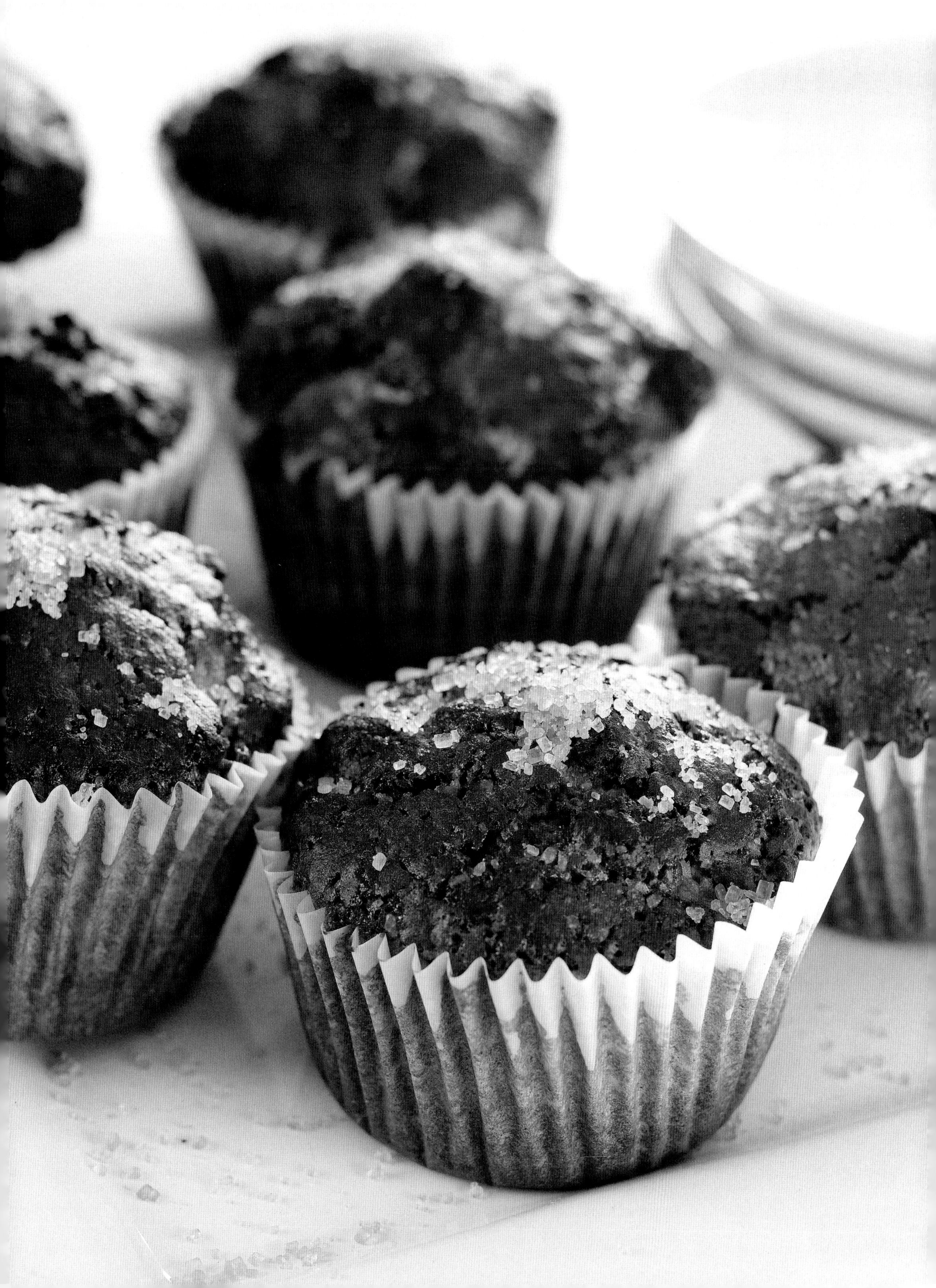

Chocolate muffins

Buttermilk makes these muffins really light.

INGREDIENTS
225g (8 oz) plain flour
60g (2 oz) cocoa powder
1 tbsp baking powder
pinch of salt
115g (4oz) light soft brown sugar
150g (5½ oz) chocolate chips
250ml (9fl oz) buttermilk
6 tbsp sunflower oil
½ tsp pure vanilla extract
2 eggs

METHOD
1 Preheat the oven to 200°C (400°F/Gas 6). Line a 12-hole American-style muffin tin with paper cases and set aside.
2 Sift the flour, cocoa powder, baking powder, and salt into a large bowl. Stir in the sugar and chocolate chips, then make a well in the centre of the dry ingredients.
3 Beat together the buttermilk, oil, vanilla, and eggs and pour the mixture into the centre of the dry ingredients. Mix together lightly to make a lumpy batter. Spoon the mixture into the paper cases, filling each three-quarters full.
4 Bake for 15 minutes, or until well risen and firm to the touch. Immediately transfer the muffins to a wire rack and leave to cool.

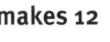

makes 12

prep 10 mins,
plus cooling
• cook 15 mins

12-hole American-
style muffin tin
• paper cases

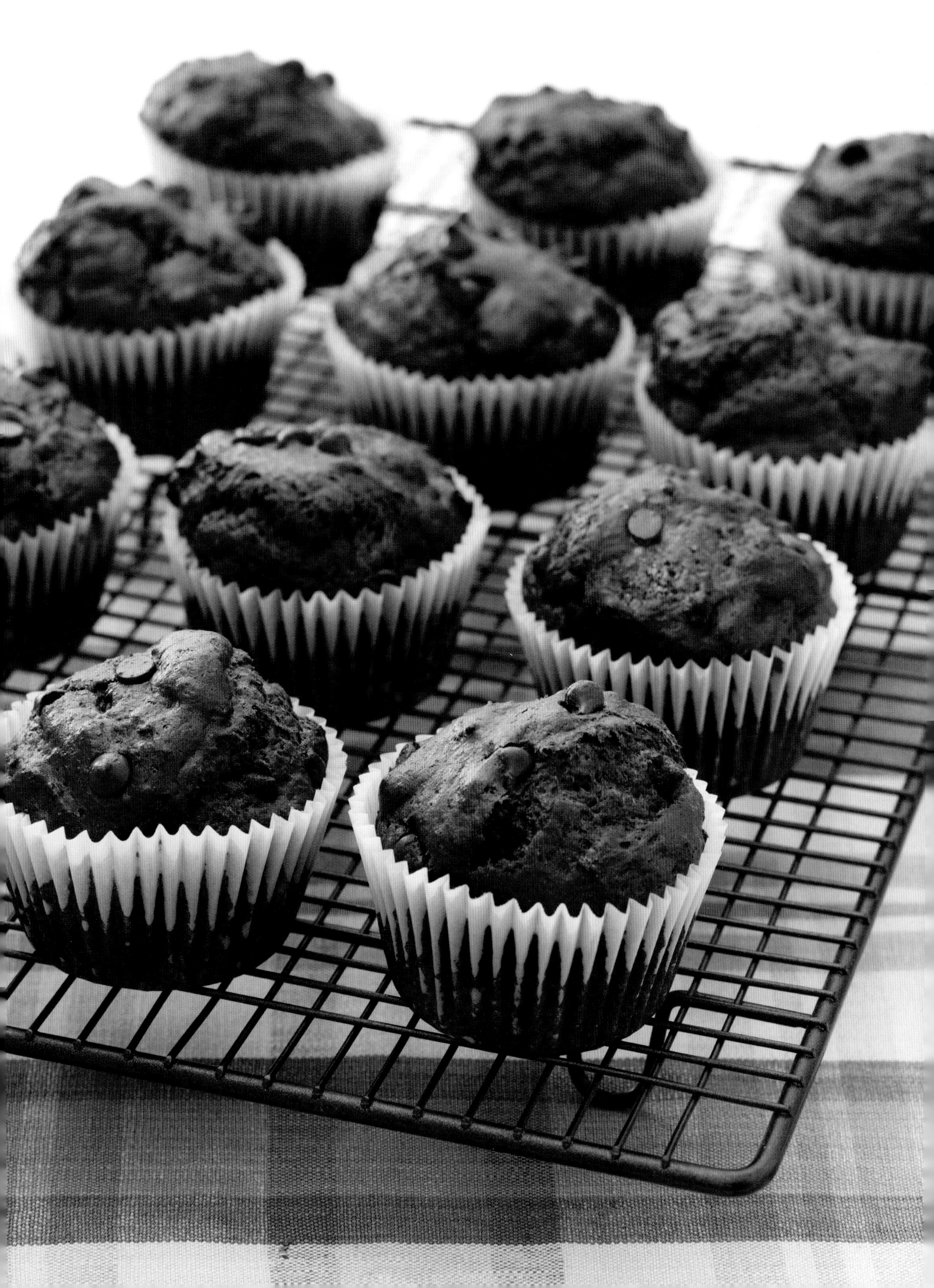

Lemon poppy seed muffins

These muffins are delightful served with brunch or as a teatime treat.

INGREDIENTS

400g (14 oz) plain white flour
1½ tsp baking powder
½ tsp baking soda
¼ tsp salt
100g (3½ oz) caster sugar
2½ tbsp poppy seeds, black or white
finely grated zest of 2 large lemons
2 eggs
250ml (9fl oz) soured cream
60g (2 oz) butter, melted and cooled
4 tbsp sunflower oil
icing sugar, for dusting

METHOD

1 Preheat the oven to 200°C (400°F/Gas 6). Line a 12-hole American-style muffin tin with paper cases and set aside. Sift the flour, baking powder, baking soda, and salt into a bowl. Stir in sugar, poppy seeds, and lemon zest, then make a well in the centre of the dry ingredients.

2 In a separate bowl, beat the eggs. Mix in the soured cream, butter, and oil and pour the mixture into the centre of the dry ingredients. Mix together lightly to make a lumpy batter. Spoon the mixture into the paper cases, filling each case three-quarters full.

3 Bake the muffins for 20 minutes, or until well risen and a fine skewer inserted in to the centre comes out clean. Sift icing sugar over the tops while still warm.

makes 12

**prep 10 mins
• cook 20 mins**

**12-hole American-style muffin tin
• paper cases**

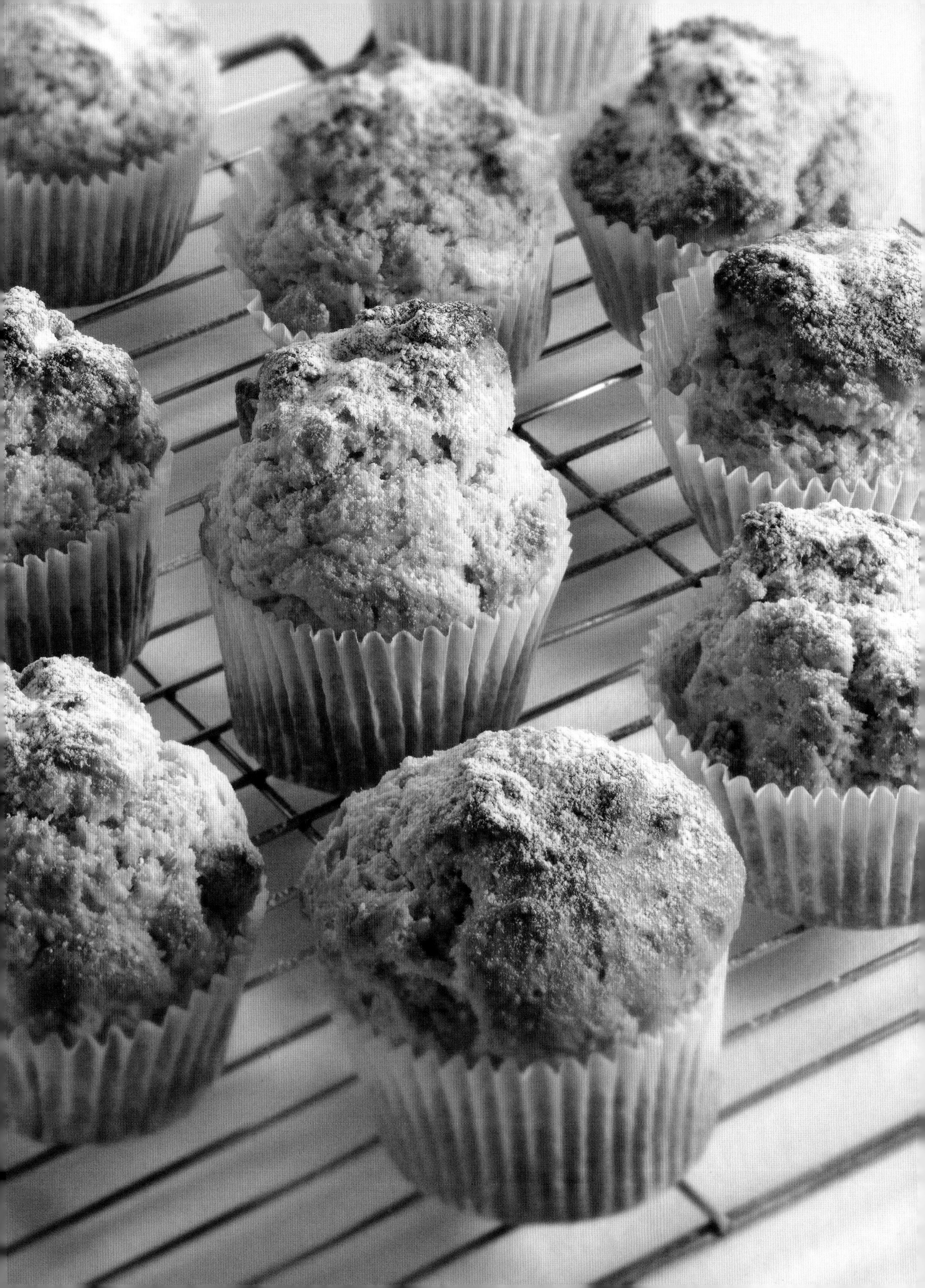

Chocolate brownies

Slightly soft in the centre, these make a tempting teatime treat.

INGREDIENTS

50g (1¾ oz) dark chocolate, chopped
25g (scant 1 oz) butter
3 eggs
1 tbsp clear honey
225g (8 oz) light soft brown sugar
75g (2½ oz) self-raising flour
175g (6 oz) walnut pieces
25g (scant 1 oz) white chocolate,
  chopped

METHOD

1 Preheat the oven to 160°C (325°F/Gas 3). Lightly grease or line a 20cm (8in) deep square cake tin with greaseproof paper.
2 Put the dark chocolate and butter into a small heatproof bowl over a saucepan of simmering water and melt, stirring occasionally. Don't let the bowl touch the water. Remove the bowl from the pan and set aside to cool slightly.
3 Beat the eggs, honey, and brown sugar together, then gradually beat in the melted chocolate mixture. Sift the flour over, add the walnut pieces and white chocolate to the bowl, and gently fold the ingredients together. Pour the mixture into the prepared tin.
4 Put the tin in the oven and bake for 30 minutes. Cover loosely with foil and bake for a further 45 minutes. The centre should be a little soft. Leave to cool completely in the tin on a wire rack.
5 When cold, invert the brownies on to a board, remove the tin, and cut into squares using a serrated knife (to cut through the nuts).

makes 16

prep 10 mins
• cook 1 hr 15 mins

20cm (8in) deep
square tin

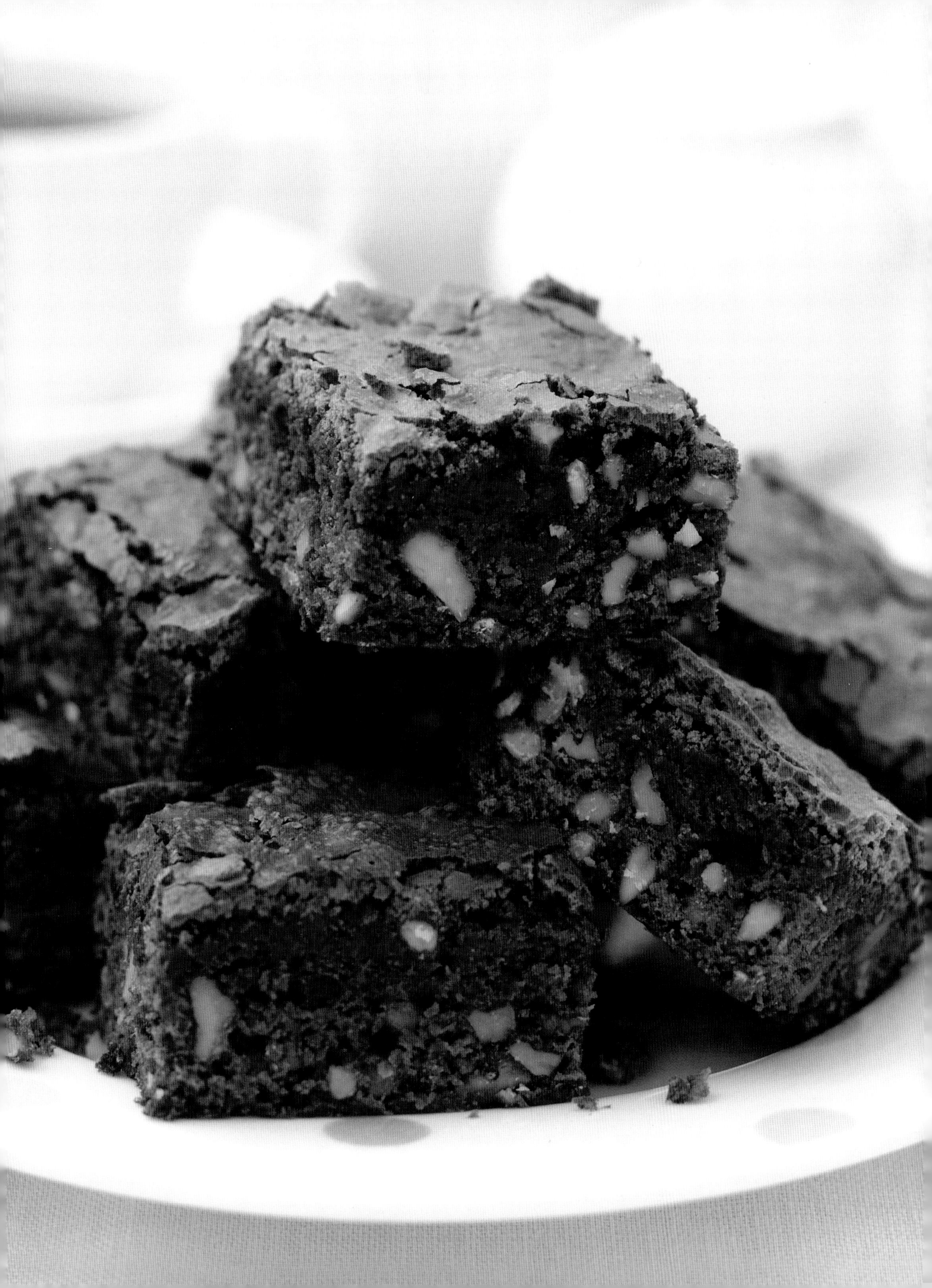

White chocolate and macadamia nut blondies

A white chocolate version of the ever-popular brownie.

INGREDIENTS
300g (10 oz) white chocolate, chopped
175g (6 oz) butter, cubed
300g (10 oz) caster sugar
4 large eggs
225g (8 oz) plain flour
100g (3½ oz) macadamia nuts, roughly
  chopped

METHOD
1 Preheat the oven to 200°C (400°F/Gas 6). Line the base and sides of the tin with baking parchment. In a bowl set over a pan of simmering water, melt the chocolate and butter together, stirring now and again until smooth. Remove, and leave to cool for about 20 minutes.

2 Once the chocolate has melted, mix in the sugar (the mixture may well become thick and grainy, but the eggs will loosen the mixture). Using a balloon whisk, stir in the eggs one at a time, making sure each is well mixed in before you add the next. Sift in the flour, fold it in, and then stir in the nuts. Pour the mixture into the tin and gently spread it out into the corners. Bake for 20 minutes, or until just firm to the touch on top but still soft underneath. Leave to cool completely in the tin, then cut into 24 squares, or rectangles for bigger blondies.

makes 24

prep 25 mins
• cook 20 mins

22 x 30cm
(8¾ x 12in) tin

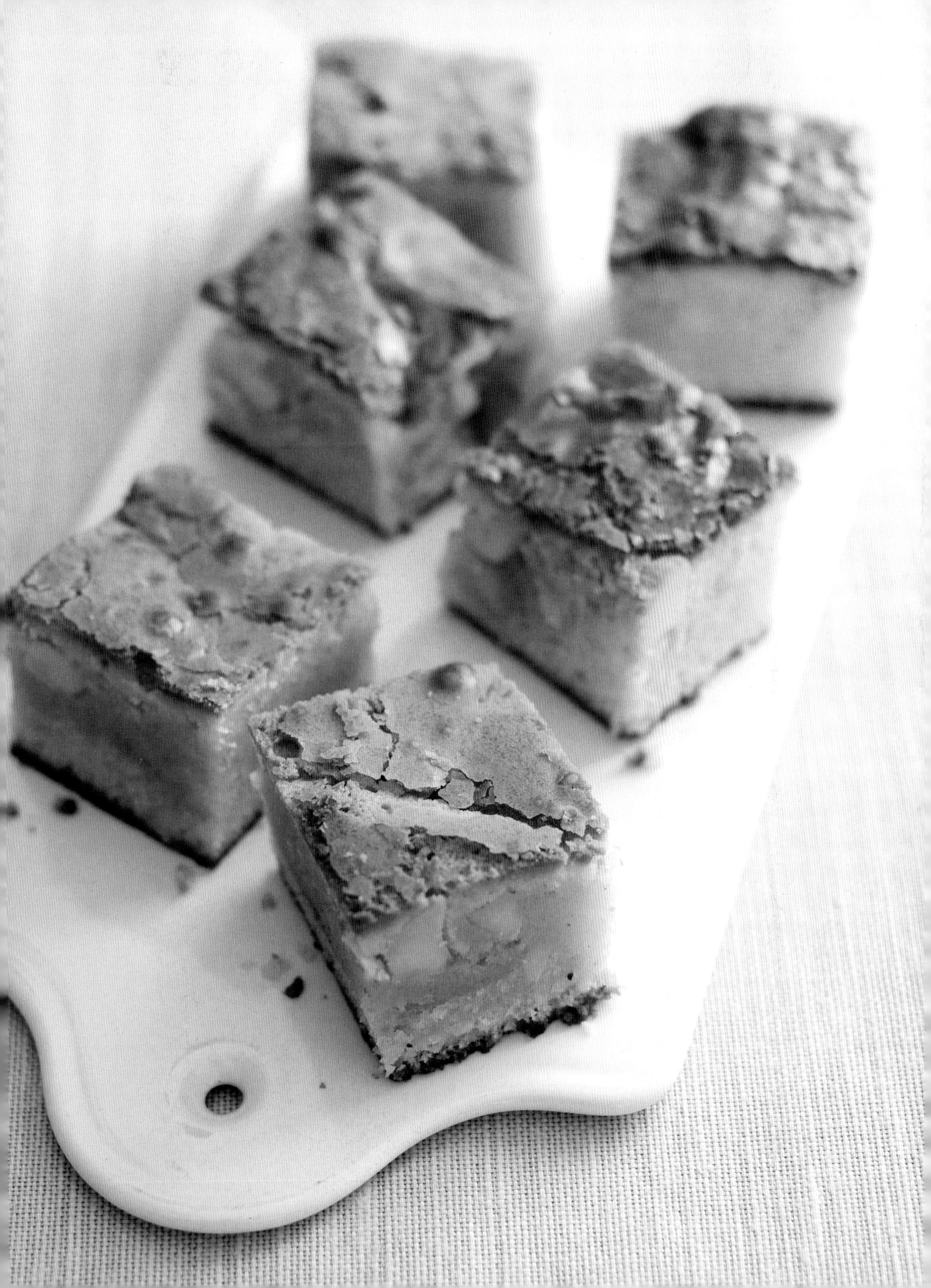

Madeleines

These little treats were made famous by writer the Marcel Proust.

INGREDIENTS

60g (2 oz) butter, melted but not hot,
  plus extra for greasing
60g (2 oz) caster sugar
2 eggs
1 tsp pure vanilla extract
60g (2 oz) self-raising flour, sifted
icing sugar, to dust

METHOD

1 Preheat the oven to 180°C (350°F/Gas 4). Carefully brush the moulds with melted butter and dust with flour.

2 Put the sugar, eggs, and vanilla extract into a mixing bowl and whisk until the mixture is pale, thick, and will hold a trail. This should take 5 minutes with an electric whisk, or slightly longer if you are using a hand whisk.

3 Sift the flour over the top and pour the melted butter down the side of the mixture. Using a large metal spoon, fold them in carefully and quickly, being careful not to knock out any air.

4 Fill the moulds with the mixture and bake in the oven for 10 minutes. Remove from the oven and transfer to a wire rack to cool, before dusting with icing sugar.

makes 12

prep 15–20 mins,
plus cooling
• cook 10 mins

madeleine tin or
12-hole bun tin

freeze for up to
1 month

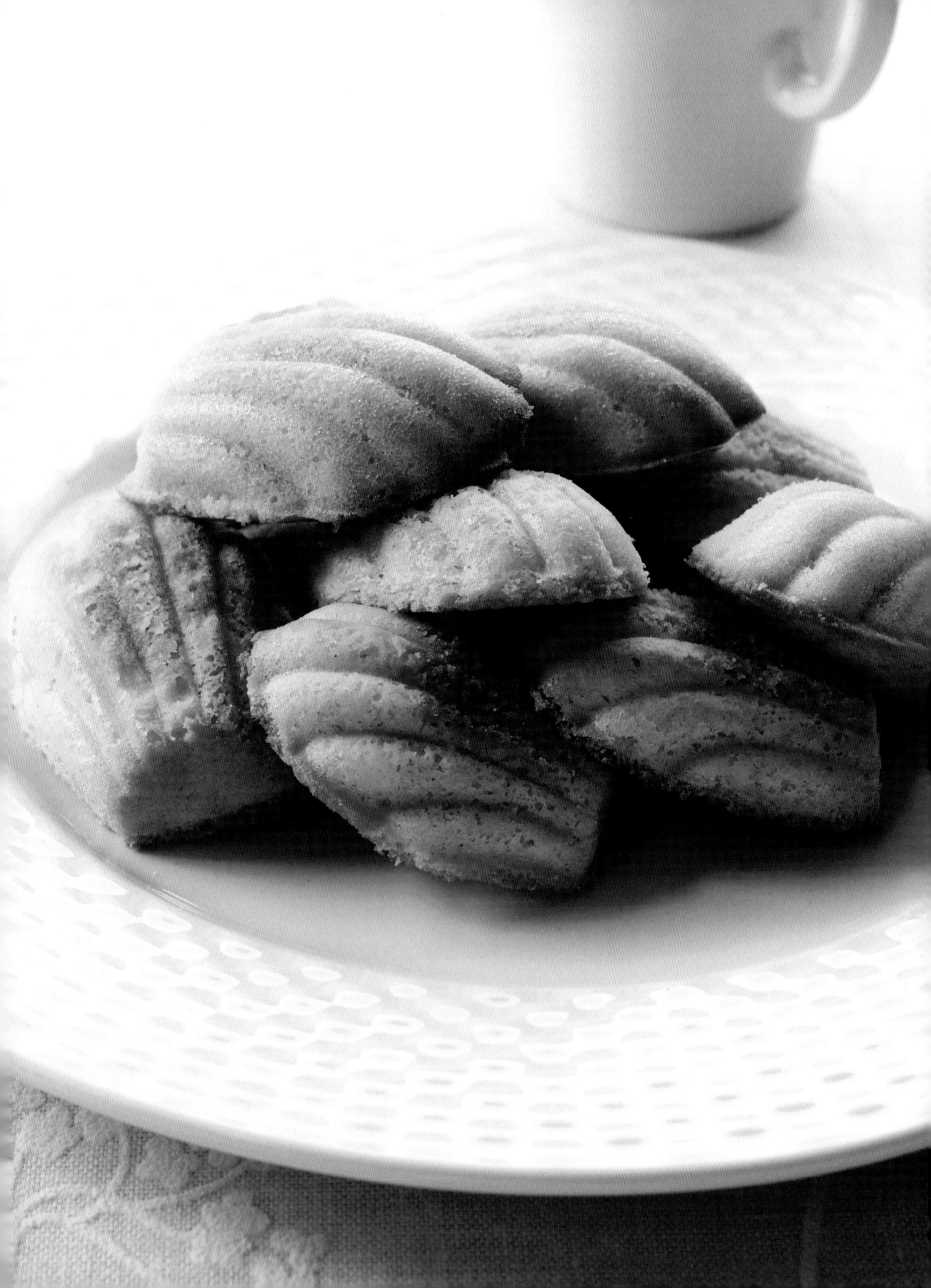

Triple chocolate crunch bars

This triple dose of dark, milk, and white chocolates should be enough to satisfy any chocoholic.

INGREDIENTS

250g (9 oz) butter, softened
200g (7 oz) caster sugar
3 medium eggs, lightly beaten
200g (7 oz) self-raising flour
50g (1¾ oz) cocoa powder
50g (1¾ oz) dark chocolate, chopped
50g (1¾ oz) milk chocolate, chopped
50g (1¾ oz) white chocolate, chopped

METHOD

1 Preheat the oven to 200°C/400°F/Gas Mark 6. Grease a baking tin with butter and line with greaseproof paper.

2 Cream the butter and sugar in a bowl using an electric hand whisk until pale and creamy. Add the eggs a little at a time, beating continuously. Fold in the flour, cocoa powder, and all the chocolate, and spread into the prepared tin.

3 Bake for 20–25 minutes until the sides have set and the centre is still a little sticky. Remove from the oven, cover with foil, and allow to cool before cutting into bars.

serves 8

prep 5 mins,
plus cooling
• cook 20–25 mins

• electric
hand whisk

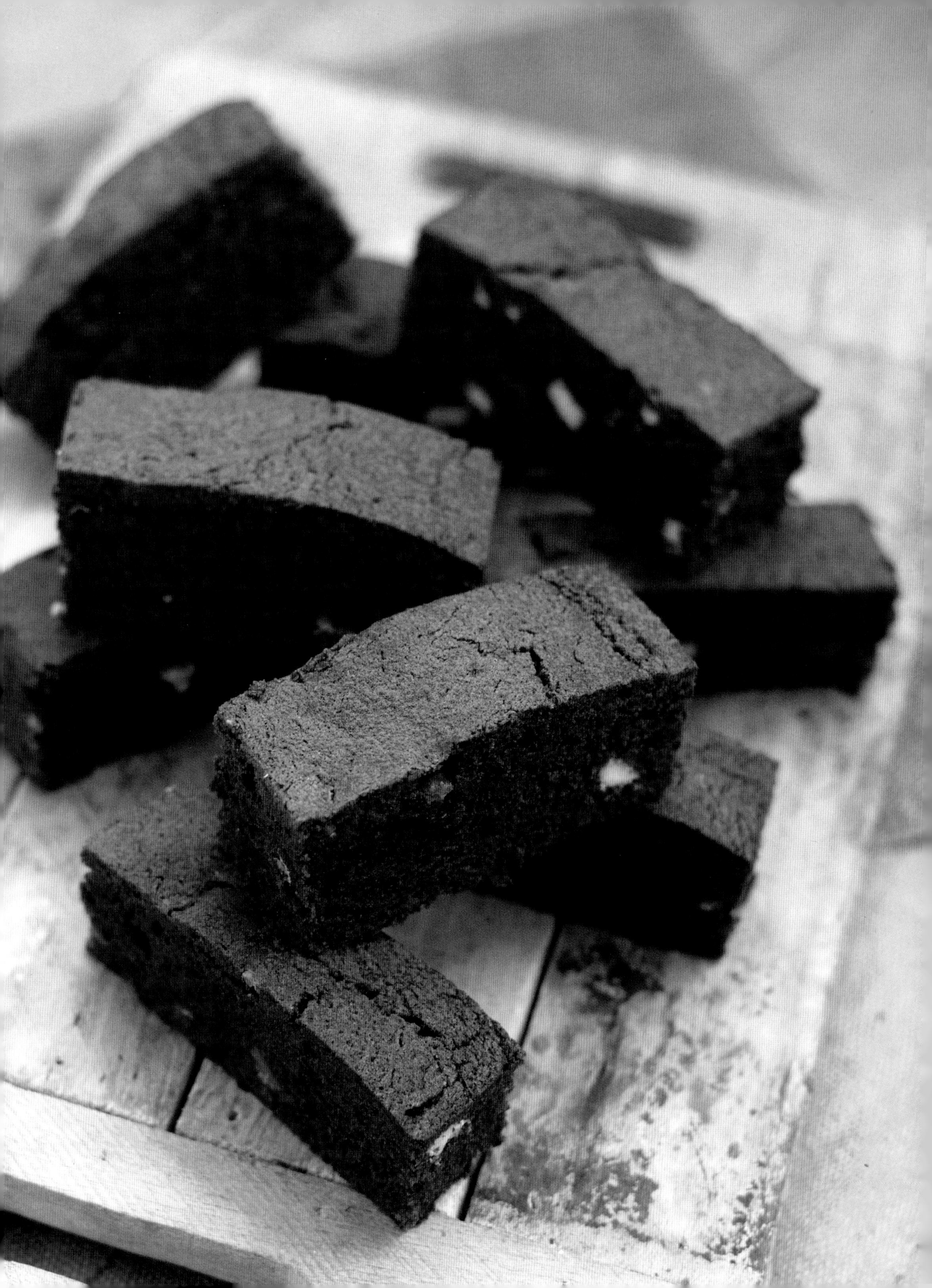

French almond financiers

So-called because these cakes are said to resemble gold bars.

INGREDIENTS

butter, for greasing

30g (1 oz) plain flour, plus extra for
  dusting

60g (2 oz) ground almonds

85g (3 oz) icing sugar, sifted

pinch of salt

85g (3 oz) unsalted butter, plus extra for
  greasing

3 egg whites

½ tsp pure vanilla extract

METHOD

1 Preheat the oven to 200°C (400°F/Gas 6). Grease the moulds or cake tin holes
  well with butter, and dust with flour.

2 Mix the almonds, icing sugar, flour, and salt together. Melt the butter, but do not let
  it get too hot. In a separate, clean bowl, whisk the egg whites until frothy, but not too
  thick. Add to the almond mixture with the butter and vanilla extract, and fold in.

3 Half-fill the greased moulds, and bake in the centre of the oven for 10–12 minutes,
  or until they have risen a little, and are golden and springy to the touch. Allow to
  cool in the moulds for 5 minutes, then carefully remove and allow to cool completely
  on a wire rack.

makes 12

**prep 15 mins,
plus cooling
• cook 10–12 mins**

**12 financier or
barquette
moulds, or a
12-hole cake tin**

**freeze for up to
3 months**

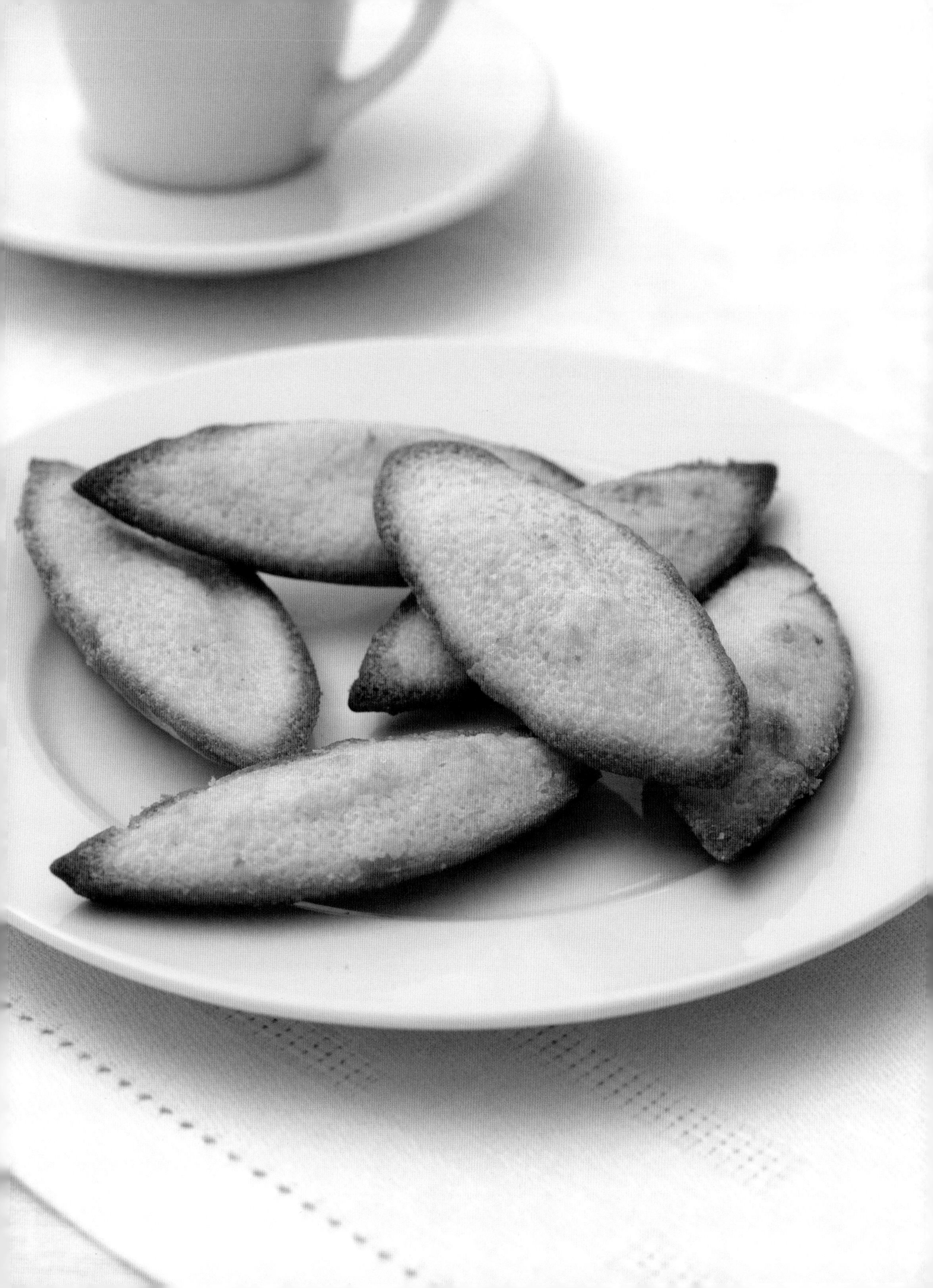

White chocolate cakes

These delicious cakes are studded with crunchy walnuts.

INGREDIENTS

50g (1¾ oz) butter, softened
50g (1¾ oz) caster sugar
1 tsp pure vanilla extract
2 medium eggs, lightly beaten
100g (3½ oz) self-raising flour
200g (7 oz) white chocolate, finely
  chopped
100g (3½ oz) walnuts, chopped

For the topping

200g (7 oz) white chocolate
50g (1¾ oz) walnuts, chopped,
  to decorate

METHOD

1 Preheat the oven to 160°C/325°F/Gas Mark 3. Grease a high-sided 16cm (7in) square tin with butter. Line with greaseproof paper and set it aside.

2 Cream the butter, sugar, and vanilla extract in a bowl with an electric hand whisk until pale and creamy. Add the eggs a little at a time, beating well after each addition. Gently fold in the flour, then the chocolate and the chopped walnuts.

3 Spread the mixture in the tin and smooth the top. Bake for 30–35 minutes, or until set. Cool in the tin for 10 minutes before turning out on to a wire rack to cool.

4 For the topping, melt the white chocolate in a heatproof bowl placed over gently simmering water, stirring until smooth and glossy. Spread it evenly over the cooled cake. Allow it to set, then decorate with chopped walnuts and cut it into 9 squares.

makes 9

prep 10 mins,
plus cooling
• cook
30–35 mins

16cm (7in) square
high-sided baking
tin • electric hand
whisk

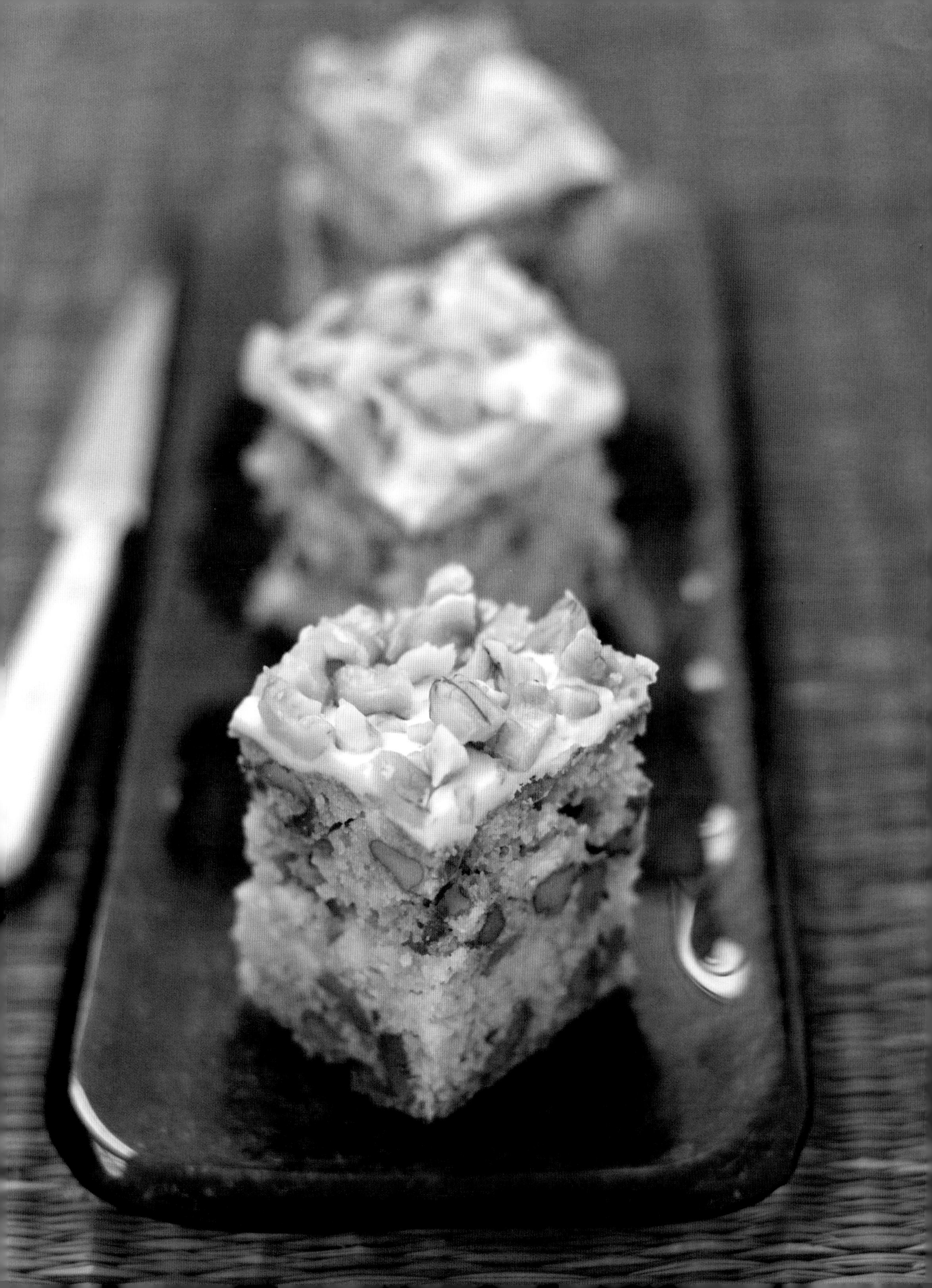

Sticky lemon cake

Fresh lemon juice and yogurt give this cake a fresh taste and moist texture.

INGREDIENTS

175g (6 oz) unsalted butter
250g (9 oz) caster sugar
2 lemons
3 eggs
75g (2½ oz) plain flour
2 tsp baking powder
150g (5½ oz) ground almonds
150g (5½ oz) natural yogurt

METHOD

1 Preheat the oven to 170°C (325°F/Gas 3). Grease the cake tin and line the base with greaseproof paper. Set aside.

2 Cream together the butter and 150g (5½ oz) caster sugar in a large bowl. Grate the zest from from both lemons, add to the bowl, and mix together.

3 Gradually beat in the eggs, one at a time. If the mixture shows signs of curdling, add 1 teaspoon of flour.

4 Mix the flour, baking powder, and ground almonds together. Sift into a separate bowl, then fold into the butter and eggs. Stir in the juice of 1 lemon and the yogurt. Pour the mixture into the tin.

5 Bake for 40 minutes or until the centre of the cake is just firm to the touch. Do not open the oven door for the first 20 minutes.

6 Remove the cake from the oven and leave to cool in the tin.

7 Heat the remaining sugar and the juice from the remaining lemon in a saucepan. Pierce the cake several times with a skewer, then drizzle the syrup over the cake. Leave to cool before removing the cake from the tin.

 serves 8

 prep 15 mins, plus cooling • cook 40 mins

 20cm (8in) deep cake tin

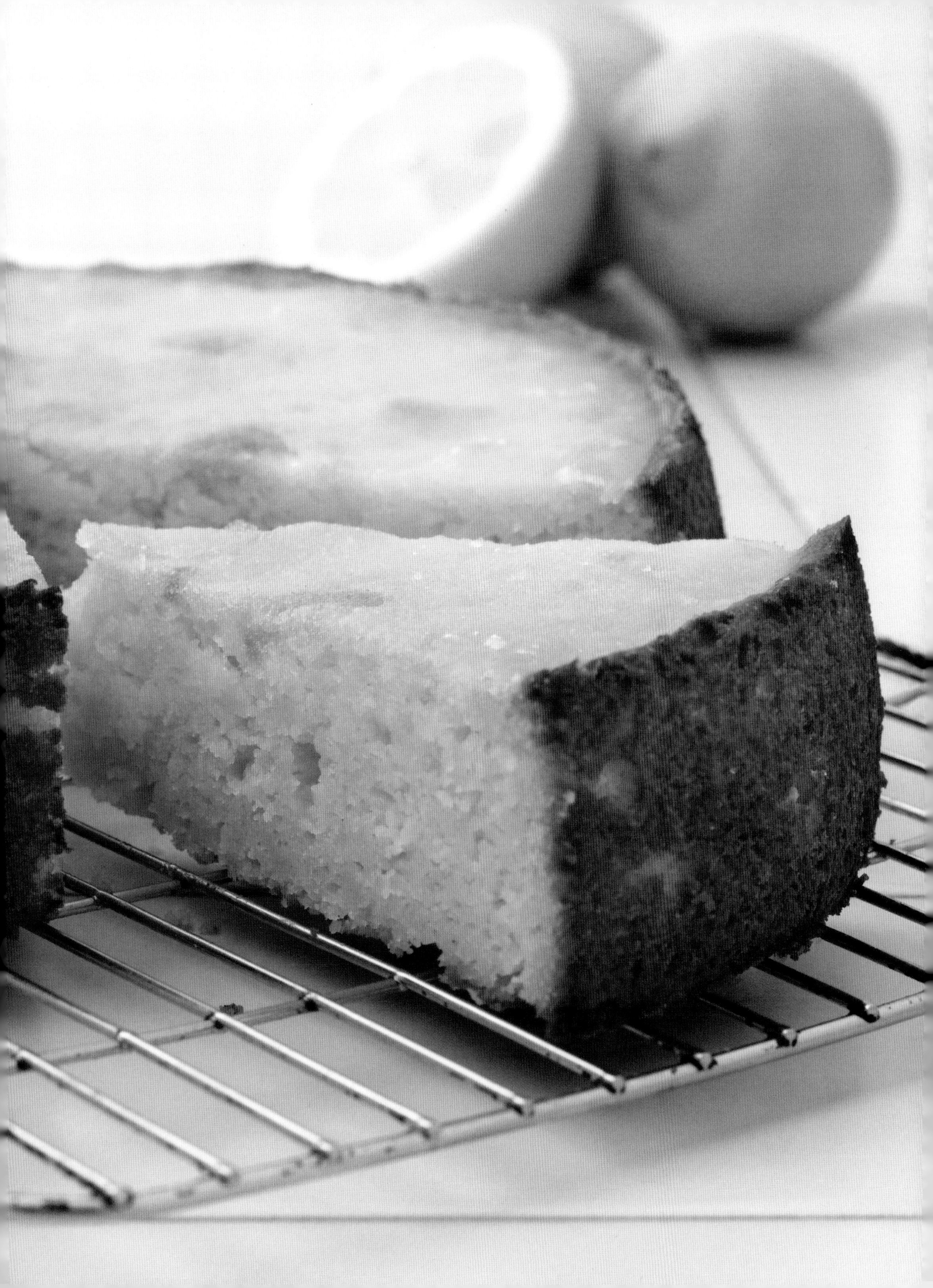

Quick carrot cake

Always popular, this cake has a hint of spice.

INGREDIENTS

75g (2½ oz) wholemeal self-raising flour
1 tsp ground allspice
½ tsp baking powder
½ tsp ground ginger
2 carrots, peeled and coarsely grated
75g (2½ oz) light soft brown sugar
50g (1¾ oz) sultanas
2 eggs, beaten
3 tbsp fresh orange juice

75g (2½ oz) unsalted butter, softened
150g (5½ oz) cream cheese
1 tbsp icing sugar
lemon zest, to garnish

METHOD

1 Preheat the oven to 190°C (375°F/Gas 5). Grease the cake tin and line the base. Sift the flour, allspice, baking powder, and ginger into a large bowl, tipping in any bran left in the sieve. Add the carrots, sugar, and sultanas, then stir to mix.

2 Add the eggs, 1 tbsp of the orange juice, and the butter. Stir together until well blended.

3 Stand the prepared tin on a baking tray, pour in the cake mixture, and level the surface using a palette knife. Bake for 20 minutes, or until a skewer inserted into the centre comes out clean. Let stand in the tin for 10 minutes, to cool.

4 Run the palette knife around the sides, invert on to a wire rack, peel off the paper, and leave to cool. Split the cake horizontally for layers.

5 Meanwhile, beat the cream cheese with the remaining orange juice and sweeten to taste with the icing sugar. Spread the icing in the centre and over the top of the cake, and decorate with lemon zest.

 serves 8

 prep 15 mins, plus cooling • cook 20 mins

 20cm (8in) cake tin

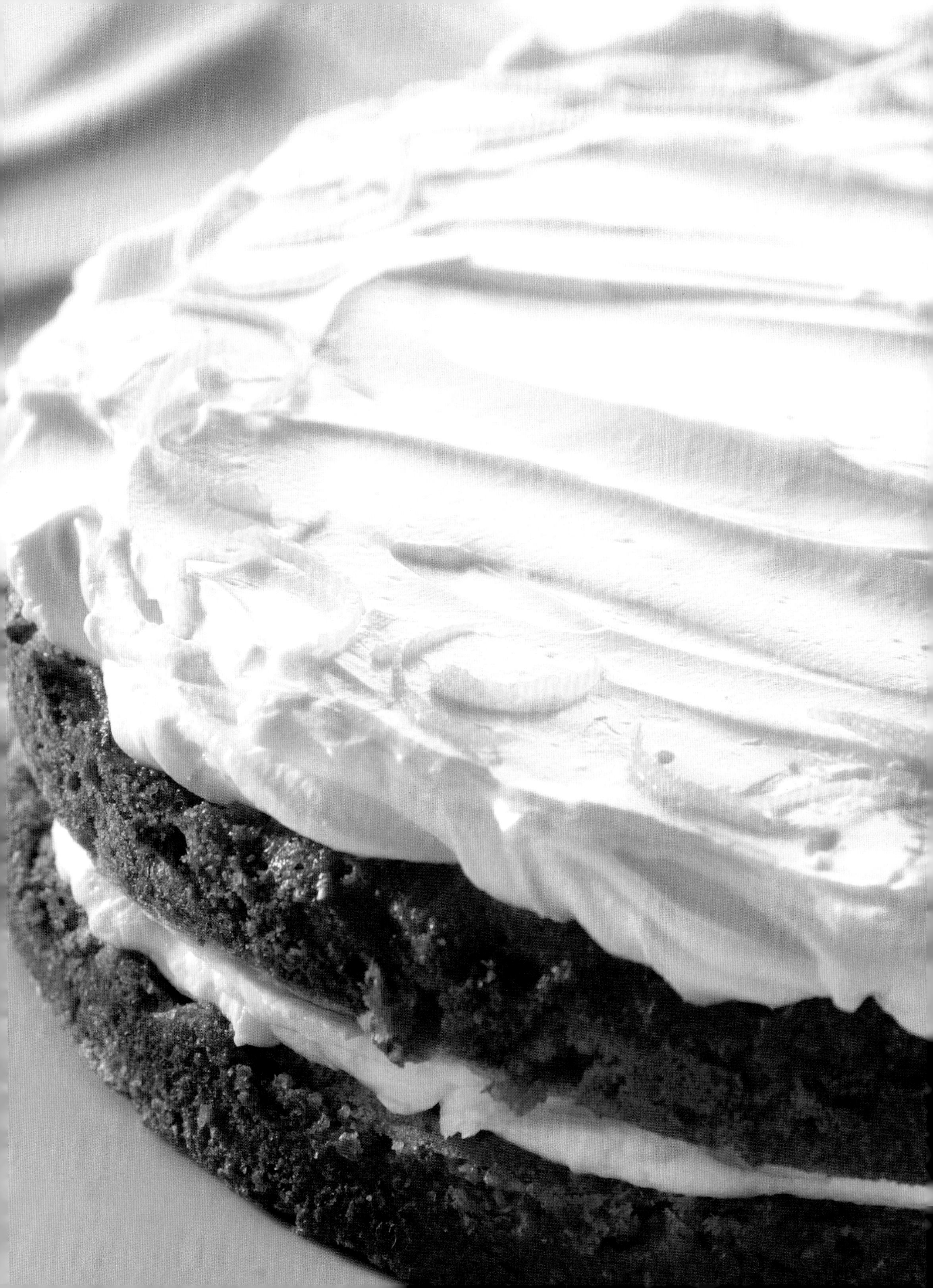

Almond and orange cake

This cake does not need flour or butter, so is great for restricted diets.

INGREDIENTS

200g (7 oz) carrots, peeled
4 large eggs, separated
few drops of pure vanilla extract
grated zest and juice of 1 orange
150g (5½ oz) caster sugar
1 tbsp orange juice, or orange-
    or almond-flavoured liqueur
150g (5½ oz) ground almonds
raspberries, to garnish
icing sugar, for dusting

METHOD

1 Preheat the oven to 160°C (325°F/Gas 3). Line the cake tin with greaseproof paper.
2 Cook the carrots in a little water until tender, then drain, cool slightly, and use a food processor or blender to blend to a purée with the orange juice.
3 Whisk the egg yolks in a large bowl with the vanilla and grated orange zest. Gradually add the sugar, whisking until it becomes thick and pale. Fold in the carrot purée and ground almonds.
4 In a clean, dry bowl, whisk the egg whites until stiff, then fold them into the yolk mixture. Pour into the prepared cake tin and bake for 1 hour, or until a skewer inserted into the centre comes out clean.
5 Cool in the tin for 10 minutes, then transfer the cake to a wire rack and leave to cool completely. Pile on the raspberries and sift icing sugar over the top to serve.

serves 8

prep 10 mins,
plus cooling
• cook 1 hr

20cm (8in) deep
cake tin • food
processor or
blender

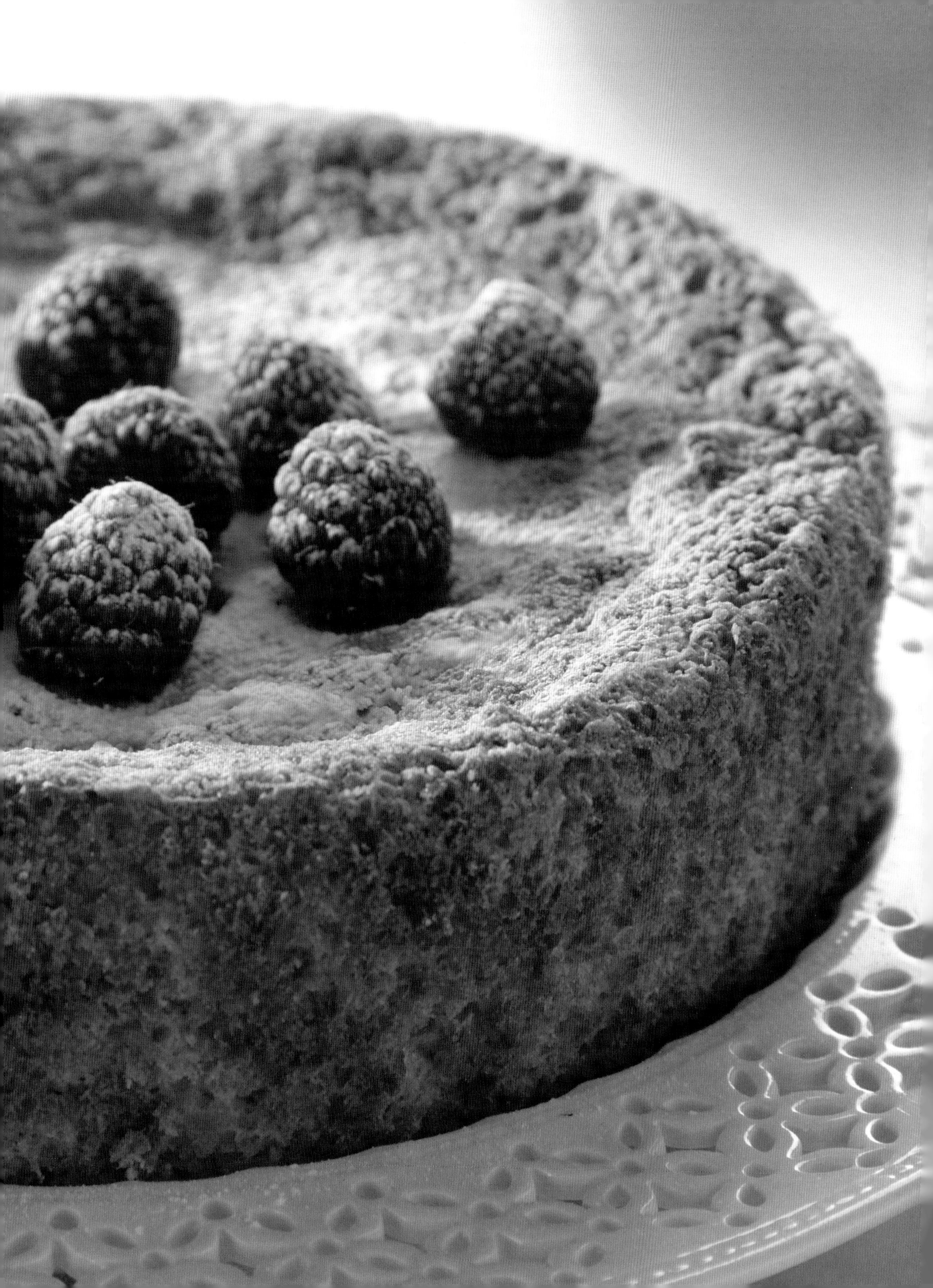

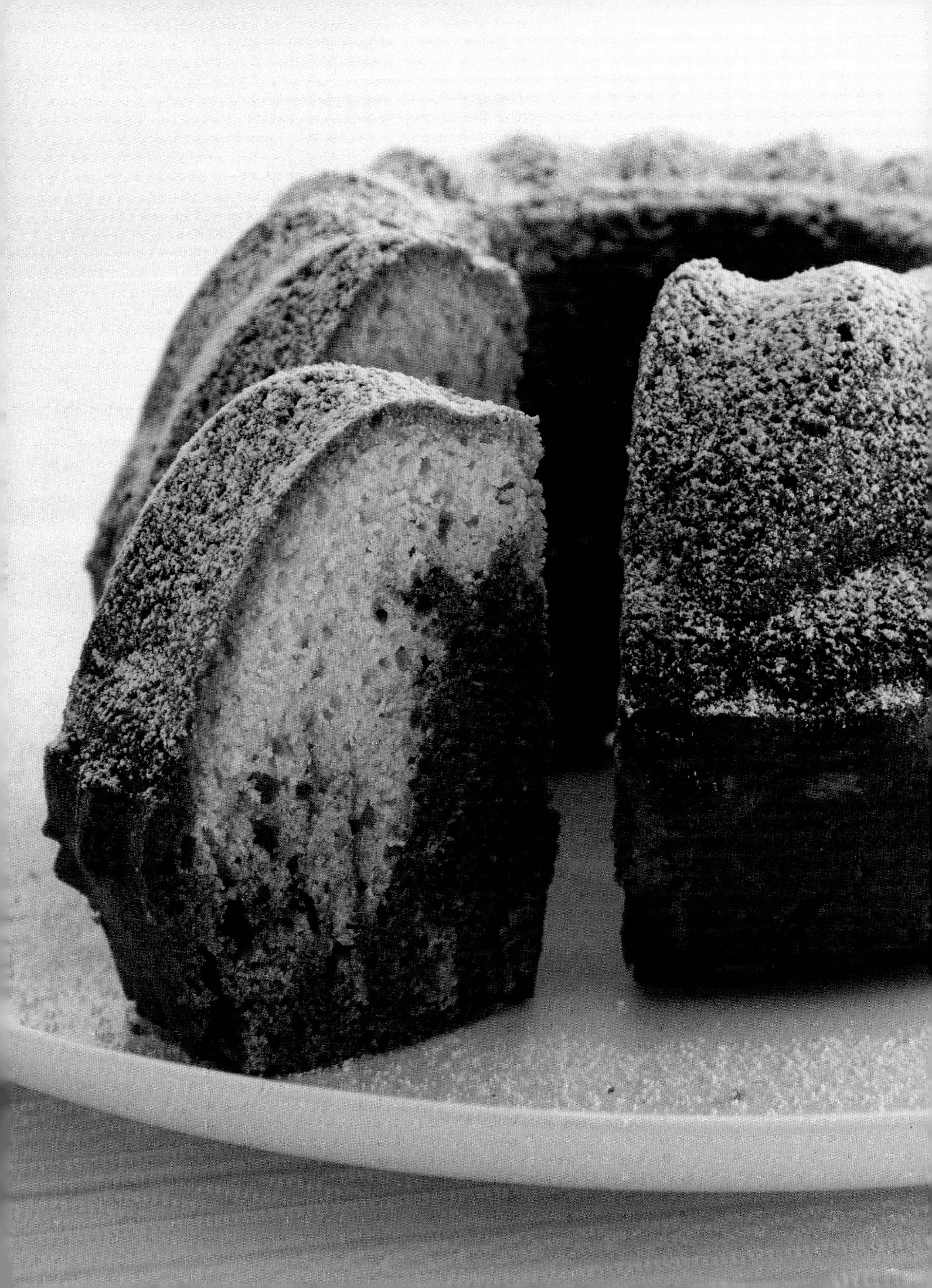

Marble cake

The marbled effect is a clever swirl of plain and chocolate batters.

INGREDIENTS

300g (10 oz) unsalted butter, softened
300g (10 oz) caster sugar
few drops of pure vanilla extract
pinch of salt
5 eggs
375g (13 oz) plain flour
4 tsp baking powder
4 tbsp milk
20g (¾ oz) cocoa powder
icing sugar, for dusting

METHOD

1 Preheat the oven to 180°C (350°F/Gas 4). Grease the kugelhopf mould or rectangular tin.
2 Place the butter in a bowl and beat until smooth. Gradually stir in the sugar, vanilla extract, and salt until thickened and smooth. Add the eggs, one at a time, whisking vigorously each time.
3 Sift the flour and baking powder into the butter and egg mixture in 2 stages, adding 2 tablespoons of the milk in between.
4 Spoon two-thirds of the mixture into the prepared tin. Sift the cocoa powder into the rest of the mixture with the remaining milk. Spoon the cocoa version on top of the plain and swirl to create a marbled pattern. Bake for 1 hour, or until risen and golden brown.
5 Leave to cool in the tin for 10 minutes, then transfer to a wire rack. Dust with icing sugar.

serves 12

prep 30 mins, plus cooling • cook 1 hr

23cm (9in) kugelhopf mould or 35 × 11cm (14 × 4½in) rectangular tin

Stollen

This rich, fruity yeast bread is traditionally served at Christmas in Germany.

INGREDIENTS

200g (7 oz) raisins
100g (3½ oz) currants
100ml (3½fl oz) rum
400g (14 oz) plain flour, plus extra for dusting
7g sachet easy-blend dried yeast
60g (2 oz) caster sugar
100ml (3½fl oz) milk

few drops of pure vanilla extract
pinch of salt
½ tsp ground mixed spice
2 eggs
175g (6 oz) butter, softened
200g (7 oz) mixed candied peel
100g (3½ oz) ground almonds
icing sugar, for dusting

METHOD

1 Put the raisins and currants into a bowl, pour over the rum, and leave to soak overnight.

2 The following day, sift the flour into a large bowl, make a well in the centre, sprinkle in the yeast, and add 1 teaspoon of the sugar. Gently heat the milk until lukewarm, and pour on top of the yeast. Leave to stand at room temperature for 15 minutes, or until frothy.

3 Add the rest of the sugar, the vanilla extract, salt, mixed spice, eggs, and butter. Using a wooden spoon, or hand-mixer with a dough hook, mix, then knead the ingredients together for 5 minutes, or until they form a smooth dough.

4 Transfer to a lightly floured work surface. Add the candied peel, soaked raisins and currants, and ground almonds to the dough, kneading for a few minutes, or until evenly incorporated. Return the dough to the bowl, cover with cling film or a damp tea towel, and leave to rise in a warm place until it has doubled in size.

5 Preheat the oven to 160°C (325°F/Gas 3). Line a baking tray with greaseproof paper. On a floured surface, roll out the dough to make a 30 x 25cm (12 x 10in) rectangle. Fold 1 long side over, just beyond the middle, then fold over the other long side to overlap the first, curling it over slightly on top to create the stollen shape. Transfer to the baking tray, and put in a warm place to rise again until doubled in size.

6 Bake in the oven for 50 minutes, or until risen and pale golden. Transfer to a wire rack to cool completely, then generously dust with icing sugar. Serve cut into thick slices, with or without butter.

makes 1 loaf

prep 35 mins, plus soaking, resting, rising, and cooling • cook 50 mins

soak the raisins and currants overnight

freeze for up to 1 month; thaw and dust with icing sugar before serving

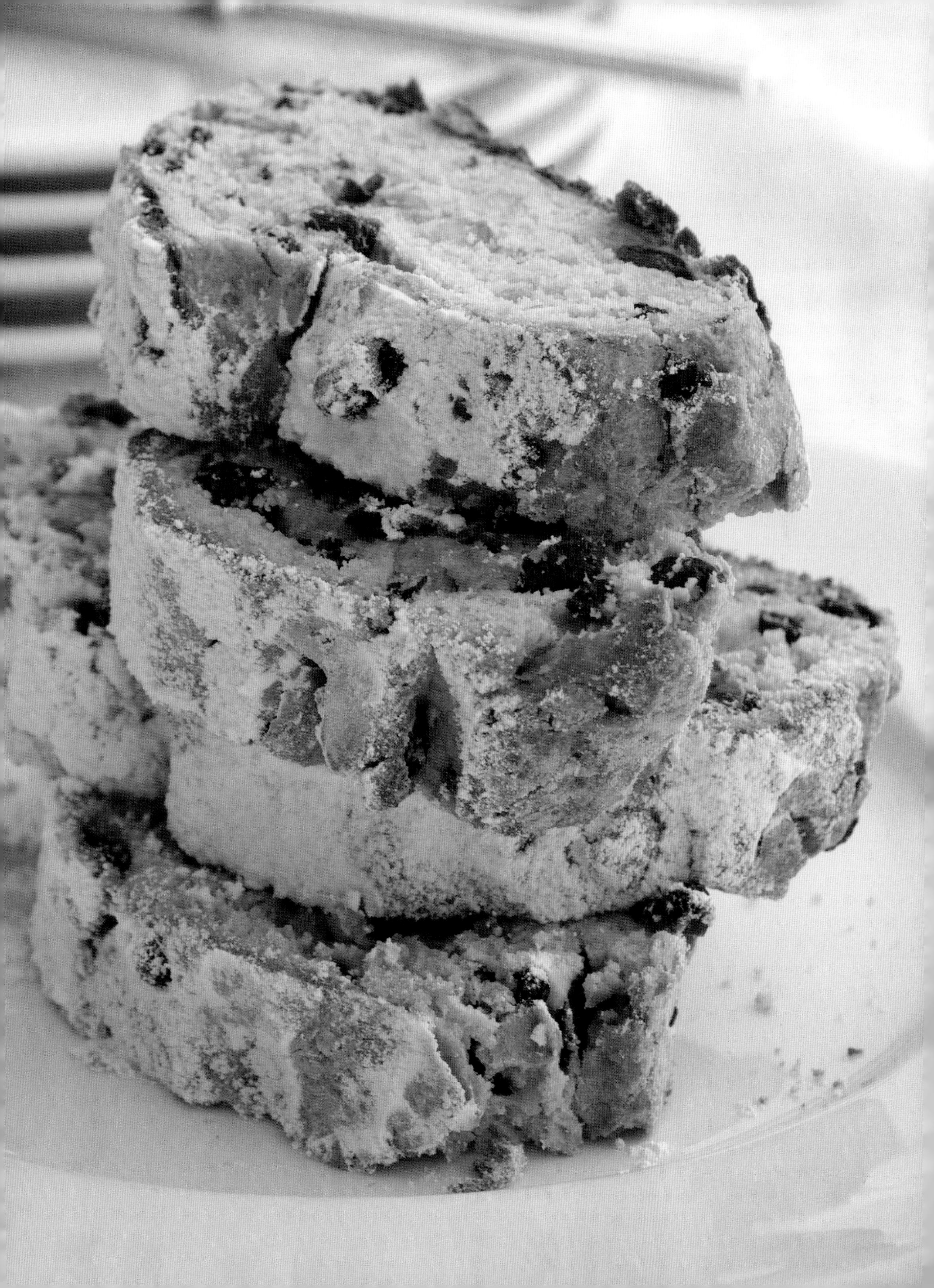

Sachertorte

INGREDIENTS

250g (9 oz) unsalted butter, softened
250g (9 oz) caster sugar
250g (9 oz) dark chocolate, melted
½ tsp pure vanilla extract
5 eggs, separated
250g (9 oz) plain flour
6–8 tbsp apricot glaze, or sieved apricot jam

For the chocolate glaze
300ml (10fl oz) whipping cream
200g (7 oz) dark chocolate, chopped
few drops of pure vanilla extract

METHOD

1   Preheat the oven to 180°C (350°F/Gas 4). Line the cake tin with greaseproof paper.

2   To make the cake, beat together the butter and the sugar until the mixture is light and fluffy, then beat in the chocolate and vanilla extract. Beat in the egg yolks, one at a time, then fold in the plain flour.

3   In a separate, clean large bowl, whisk the egg whites until stiff. Spoon a little of the egg whites into the chocolate mixture, and mix in to lighten it slightly, then carefully fold in the remaining egg whites. Pour the mixture into the lined cake tin and level the surface.

4   Bake the cake in the centre of the oven for 45–60 minutes, or until it feels just firm to the touch in the centre and a skewer inserted into it comes out clean. Remove from the oven, and place the tin on a wire rack. Leave the cake to cool in the tin.

5   To make the chocolate glaze, pour the cream into a small saucepan, and bring it to the boil. Place the chopped chocolate in a bowl, then pour in the cream, and stir until the chocolate melts. Add a few drops of vanilla extract. Leave the chocolate mixture to cool slightly, until it reaches a coating consistency, stirring occasionally. If the glaze cools too much and becomes too thick, it can be gently re-warmed.

6   Heat the apricot glaze in a small saucepan until runny. Slice the cake in half horizontally, and spread half with a thin layer of the apricot glaze, then sandwich the 2 halves together again. Spread the remaining glaze over the top and sides of the cake.

7   Place the cake on a wire rack over a plate or tray. Reserve 3 tablespoons of the glaze. Pour the rest of the glaze over the cake, using a palette knife to spread it evenly over the sides. Any glaze that runs off on to the plate or tray may be re-used. Leave the cake in a cool place until the glaze has set.

8   Beat the reserved glaze briefly, re-warming it slightly if it is very thick, then use it to fill a piping bag fitted with a plain nozzle. Pipe the word "Sacher" across the top of the cake.

serves 8–12

prep 40 mins,
plus cooling
• cook 45–60 mins

23cm (9in)
round cake tin
• palette knife
• piping bag

freeze,
undecorated, for
up to 3 months

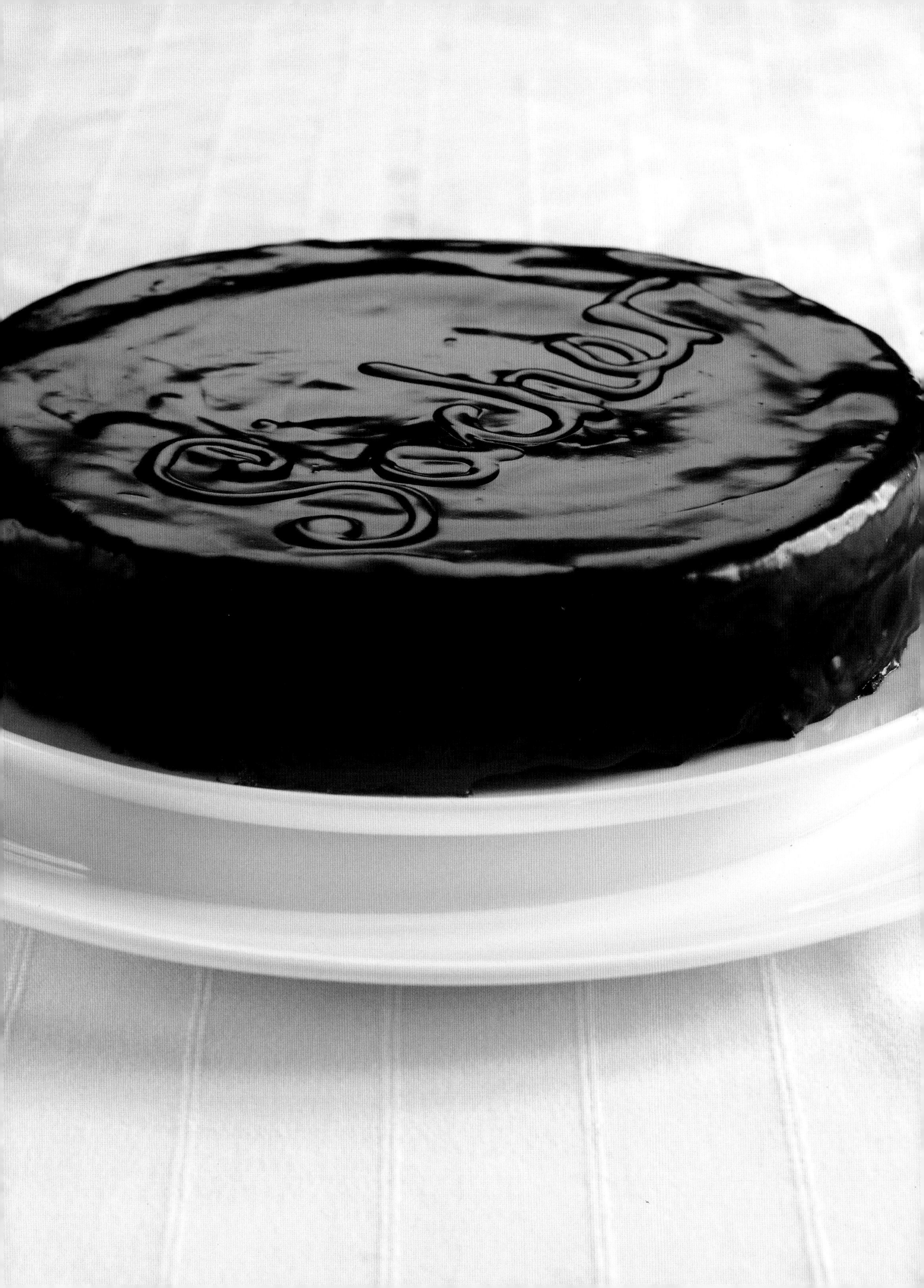
Sacher

Panforte

This famous cake from Siena, Italy, dates from the 13th century.

INGREDIENTS

rice paper, for lining
115g (4 oz) whole blanched almonds, toasted and roughly chopped
125g (4½ oz) hazelnuts, toasted and roughly chopped
200g (7 oz) mixed candied orange and lemon peel, chopped
115g (4 oz) dried figs, roughly chopped
finely grated zest of 1 lemon
½ tsp ground cinnamon
½ tsp freshly grated nutmeg
¼ tsp ground cloves
¼ tsp ground allspice
75g (2½ oz) rice flour or plain flour
30g (1 oz) unsalted butter
140g (5 oz) caster sugar
4 tbsp clear honey
icing sugar, to dust

METHOD

1 Line the base and sides of the cake tin with greaseproof paper, then put a disc of rice paper on top of the paper. Preheat the oven to 180°C (350°F/Gas 4).

2 Put the almonds, hazelnuts, candied peel, figs, lemon zest, cinnamon, nutmeg, cloves, allspice, and flour in a large bowl and mix well.

3 Put the butter, caster sugar, and honey in a pan and heat gently until melted. Pour into the fruit and nut mixture and stir to combine. Spoon into the prepared tin and, with damp hands, press down to create a smooth, even layer.

4 Bake for 30 minutes, then remove from the oven, leaving it in the tin to cool and become firm. When completely cold, remove the panforte from the tin. Peel off the paper but leave the rice paper stuck to the bottom of the cake.

5 Dust heavily with icing sugar and serve cut into small wedges.

serves 12–16

prep 30 mins, plus cooling • cook 30 mins

20cm (8in) loose-bottomed cake tin

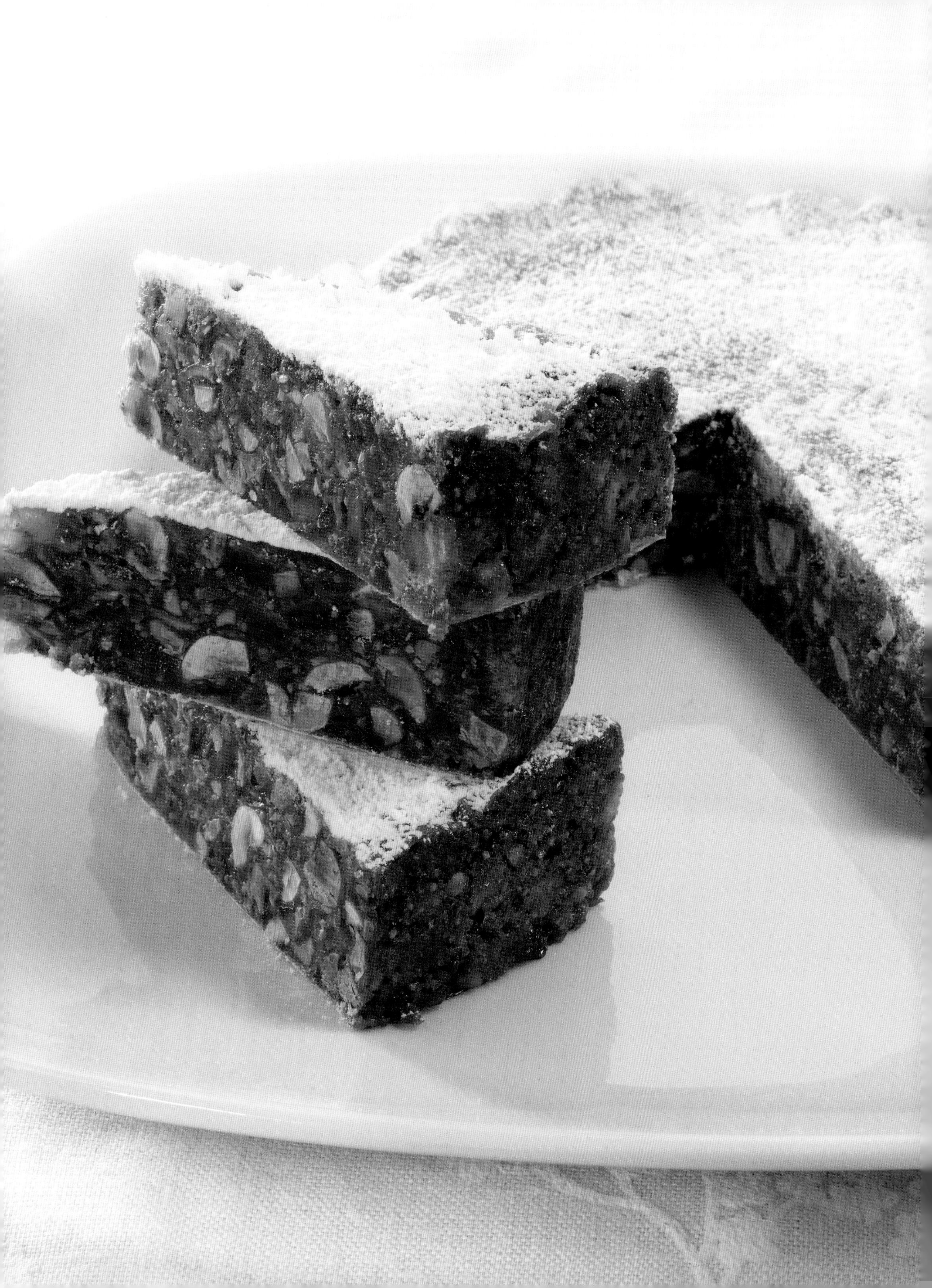

Chocolate amaretti roulade

Crushed amaretti biscuits add crunch to indulgent roulade.

INGREDIENTS

6 large eggs, separated
150g (5½ oz) caster sugar
50g (1¾ oz) cocoa powder
icing sugar, to dust
300ml (10fl oz) double cream or
  whipping cream

2–3 tbsp Amaretto or brandy
20 amaretti biscuits, crushed, plus
  2 extra
50g (1¾ oz) dark chocolate

METHOD

1 Preheat the oven to 180°C (350°F/Gas 4). Line the Swiss roll tin with baking parchment. Put the egg yolks and sugar in a large heatproof bowl set over a pan of simmering water and whisk with an electric hand whisk until very pale, thick, and creamy. This will take about 10 minutes. Remove from the heat. Put the egg whites in a mixing bowl and whisk with an electric hand whisk (and clean beaters) until soft peaks form.

2 Sift the cocoa powder into the egg yolk mixture and very gently fold in along with the egg whites. Pour into the tin and smooth into the corners. Bake for 20 minutes, or until just firm to the touch. Allow the tin to cool slightly before carefully turning the sponge out on to a sheet of baking parchment well dusted with icing sugar. Remove the tin from the sponge, but leave the parchment, and allow to cool for 30 minutes.

3 Put the cream in a mixing bowl and whisk with an electric hand whisk until soft peaks form. Peel the parchment off the sponge, trim the sides to neaten them, then drizzle over the Amaretto or brandy. Spread with the cream, scatter with the crushed amaretti biscuits, then grate over most of the chocolate.

4 Starting from one of the short sides, roll the roulade up, using the parchment to help keep it tightly together. Place on a serving plate with the join underneath. Crumble over the extra biscuits, grate over the remaining chocolate, and dust with a little icing sugar.

serves 8

prep 30 mins,
plus cooling
• cook 20 mins

23 x 33cm
(9 x 13in) Swiss
roll tin • electric
hand whisk

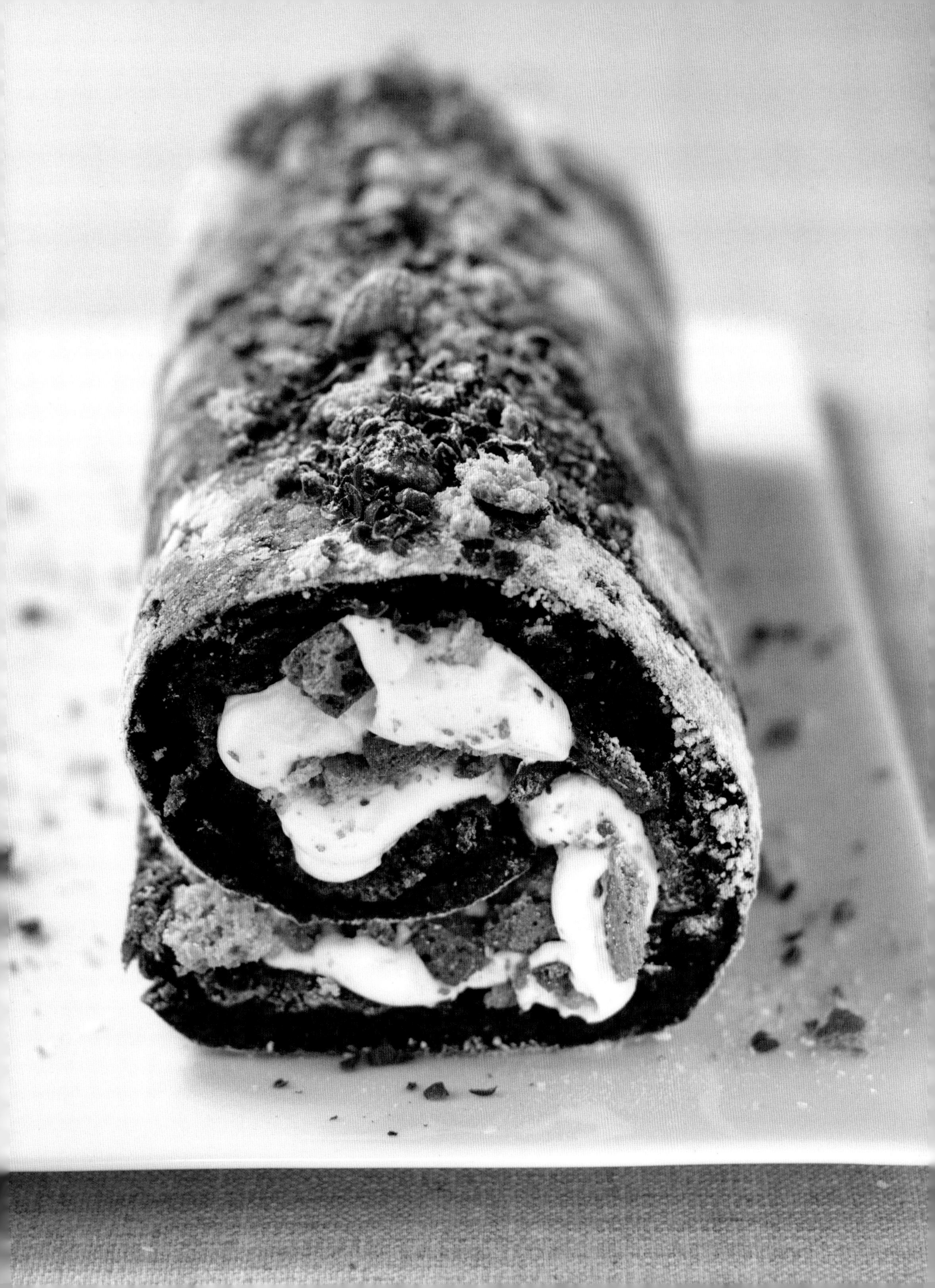

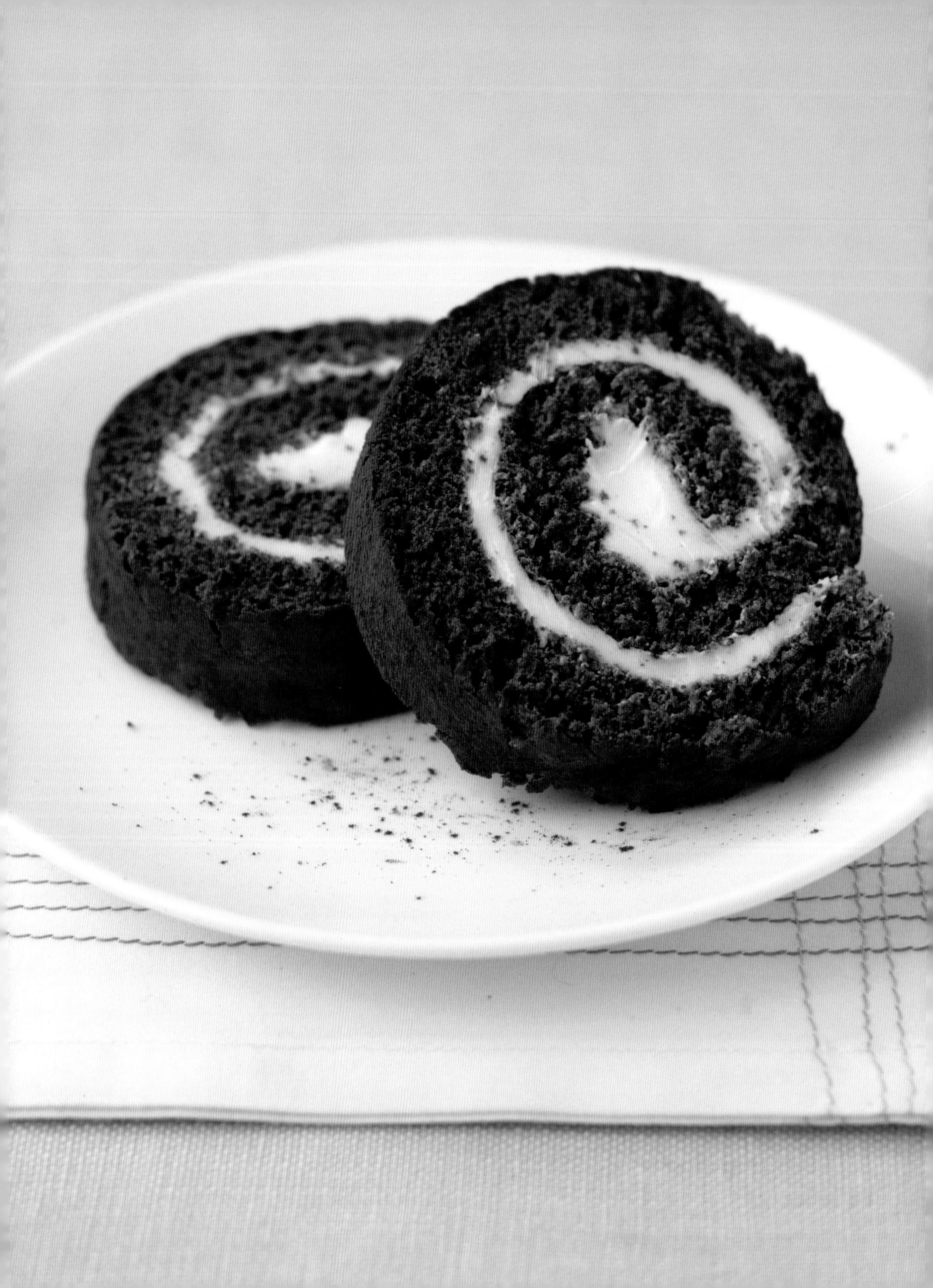

Chocolate and buttercream Swiss roll

This classic is always a hit at children's parties.

INGREDIENTS

3 large eggs
75g (2½ oz) caster sugar
50g (1¾ oz) plain flour
25g (scant 1 oz) cocoa powder, plus
  extra to dust
75g (2½ oz) butter, softened
125g (4½ oz) icing sugar

METHOD

1 Preheat the oven to 200°C (400°F/Gas 6). Sit a large heatproof bowl over a pan of simmering water, add the eggs and sugar, and whisk for 5–10 minutes or until the mixture is thick and creamy. Sift in the flour and cocoa powder and fold in gently with a metal spoon.

2 Line the Swiss roll tin with baking parchment, then pour the mixture into the tin and level the top. Bake for 10 minutes, or until the sponge is springy to the touch. Remove from the oven, cover with a damp tea towel, and leave to cool.

3 Turn the sponge out on to a sheet of greaseproof paper dusted with cocoa powder. Put the butter in a mixing bowl and beat with an electric hand whisk until creamy. Whisk in the icing sugar a little at a time, then spread the mixture over the top of the sponge. Using the greaseproof paper to help you, roll the sponge up, starting from one of the short sides. Dust with more cocoa powder, if needed, and serve.

serves 8

prep 25 mins
• cook 10 mins

20 x 30cm
(8 x 12in) Swiss
roll tin • electric
hand whisk

Celebration cake

This moist, rich fruit cake is ideal for Christmas, weddings, and christenings.

INGREDIENTS

200g (7 oz) sultanas
400g (14 oz) raisins
350g (12 oz) prunes, chopped
350g (12 oz) glacé cherries
2 small dessert apples, peeled, cored, and finely chopped
600ml (1 pint) cider
4 tsp mixed spice
200g (7 oz) unsalted butter, softened
175g (6 oz) dark brown sugar

3 eggs, beaten
150g (5½ oz) ground almonds
300g (10 oz) plain flour
2 tsp baking powder
400g ready-made marzipan icing
3 large egg whites, plus 1 extra for the berries
500g (1lb 2oz) icing sugar
mixed fresh berries, to decorate
caster sugar, for frosting

METHOD

1 Place the sultanas, raisins, prunes, glacé cherries, chopped apple, cider, and spice in a saucepan, bring slowly to simmering point over a medium-low heat, cover, and simmer for 20 minutes, or until most of the liquid has been absorbed.

2 Remove from the heat, and leave to rest overnight at room temperature.

3 Preheat the oven to 160°C (325°F/Gas 3). Double-line the cake tin with greaseproof paper. In a large bowl, cream the butter and sugar together until pale and fluffy, then add the eggs, a little at a time.

4 Fold in the fruit and nuts, then sift the flour and baking powder, and fold into the mixture.

5 Spoon the mixture into the prepared tin, cover with foil, and bake for 2½ hours, or until a skewer inserted into the centre of the cake comes out clean. Leave to cool.

6 Cover with the marzipan icing. Place the egg whites in a bowl and stir in the icing sugar. Whisk for 10 minutes until stiff, then spread on top of the marzipan. To decorate, make frosted berries by dipping fresh berries in beaten egg white, then in caster sugar, and leaving to dry.

 serves 16

 prep 25 mins, plus soaking and cooling • cook 2 hrs 30 mins

 complete steps 1–2 a day ahead to allow to soak overnight

 deep 20–25cm (8–10in) square cake tin

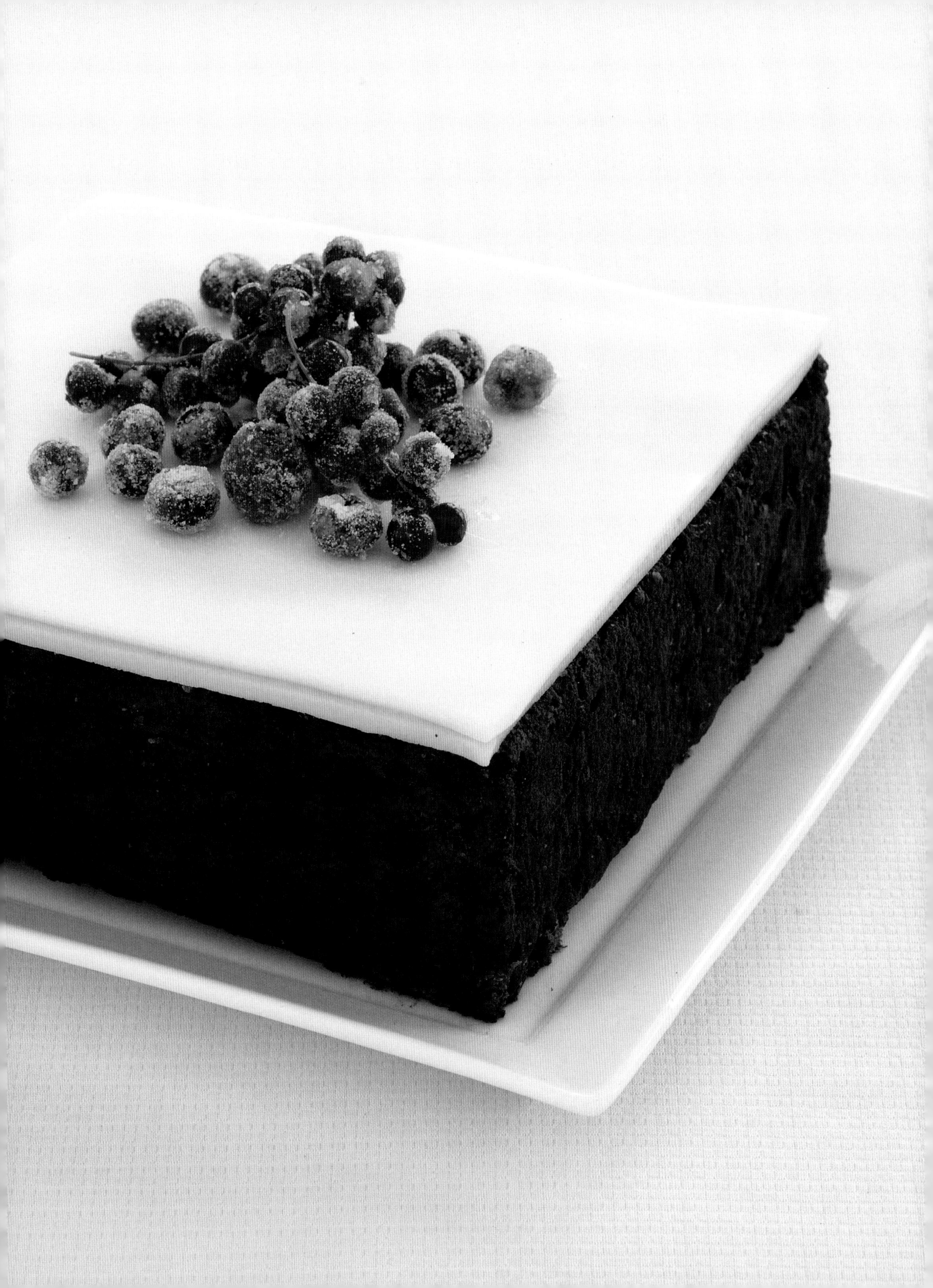

Victoria sponge cake

This English classic is a favourite that has stood the test of time.

INGREDIENTS
175g (6 oz) butter
175g (6 oz) caster sugar
3 eggs, lightly beaten
175g (6 oz) self-raising flour
6–8 tbsp raspberry jam
150ml (5fl oz) double cream
icing sugar, to dust

METHOD
1 Preheat the oven to 190°C (375°F/Gas 5). Lightly grease and line the bottom of the tins with greaseproof paper.
2 Beat the butter and sugar together until pale and fluffy. It is important to beat the mixture well at this stage to incorporate as much air as possible, which helps prevent the eggs from curdling.
3 Add the eggs a little at a time, beating well after each addition. If the mixture begins to curdle, beat in 1–2 tablespoons of the flour. Sift the flour, and fold into the egg mixture using a large metal spoon or a spatula.
4 Divide the mixture equally between the prepared tins, and spread evenly to level the tops. Bake for 20–25 minutes, until pale golden and springy to the touch. Allow the cakes to cool in the tins for 5 minutes, before turning out on to a wire rack. Peel off the lining paper, and allow to cool completely.
5 When the cakes are cool, place one upside down on a serving plate, and spread with the raspberry jam. Lightly whip the cream, until just holding its shape, and spread over the jam. Add the remaining cake, and dust lightly with icing sugar before serving.

serves 8 | prep 20 mins, plus cooling • cook 20–25 mins | for the best results, keep all ingredients at room temperature | 2 × 20cm (8in) sandwich tins | freeze for up to 1 month

Black Forest gâteau

The stunning Black Forest region of Germany is home to this indulgent cake.

INGREDIENTS

6 eggs
175g (6 oz) golden caster sugar
125g (4½ oz) plain flour
50g (1¾ oz) cocoa powder
1 tsp pure vanilla extract

85g (3 oz) butter, melted
600ml (1 pint) double cream
2 x 425g can pitted black cherries
4 tbsp Kirsch
150g (5½ oz) dark chocolate, grated

METHOD

1 Preheat the oven to 180°C (350°F/Gas 4). Lightly grease and line the bottom of the tin with greaseproof paper. Put the eggs and sugar into a large heatproof bowl, and place over a saucepan filled with simmering water. Don't let the bowl touch the water. Whisk until the mixture is pale and thick, and will hold a trail. Remove from the heat and whisk for another 5 minutes, or until cooled slightly.

2 Sift the flour and cocoa together and fold into the egg mixture using a large metal spoon or a spatula. Fold in the vanilla extract and butter. Transfer to the prepared tin and level the surface. Bake in the oven for 40 minutes, or until risen and just shrinking away a little from the sides. Turn it out on to a wire rack, discard the lining paper, and cover with a clean cloth. Allow the cake to cool completely.

3 Carefully cut the cake into three layers. Drain 1 can of cherries, placing 6 tablespoons of the juice into a bowl with the Kirsch. Roughly chop the drained cherries. Drizzle a third of the Kirsch and cherry syrup over each layer of sponge.

4 Whip the cream until it just holds its shape. Place 1 layer of the cake on to a serving plate. Spread a thin layer of cream over the top of the sponge, and scatter with half the chopped cherries. Repeat with layers and top with the final layer of sponge. Using a palette knife, spread a thin layer of cream around the edges of the cake to cover, and spoon the remaining cream into a piping bag fitted with a star-shaped nozzle.

5 Using a spoon or a palette knife, press the grated chocolate onto the side of the cake. Pipe swirls of cream around the top edge of the cake. Drain the second tin of cherries and use them to fill the centre of the cake. Scatter any remaining chocolate over the piped cream.

 serves 8

 prep 55 mins, plus cooling • cook 40 mins

 23cm (9in) springform cake tin • piping bag

 freeze for up to 1 month; defrost for 5–6 hours in the fridge

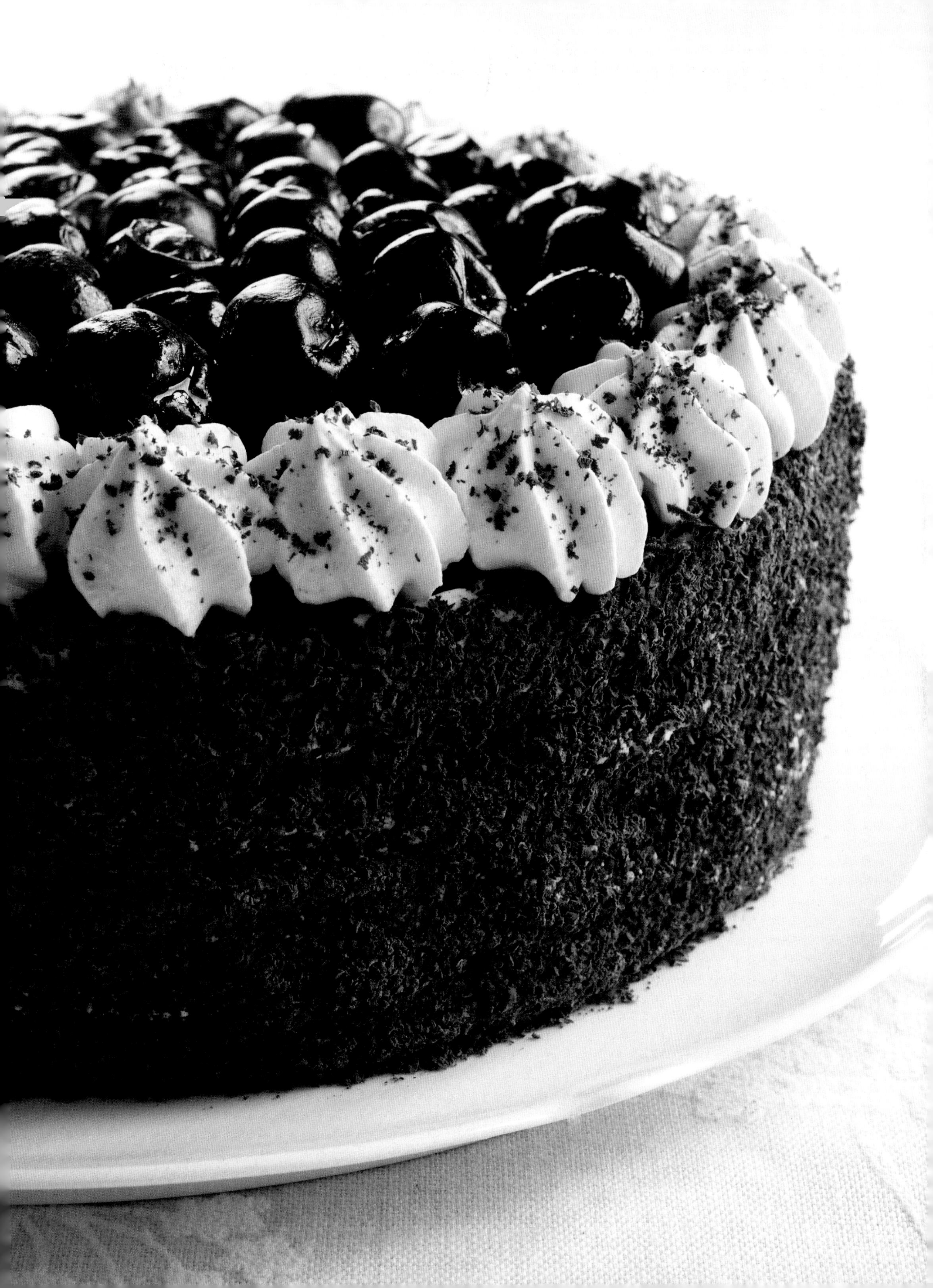

Tartuffo

This Italian chocolate truffle cake is rich, dark, and indulgent.

INGREDIENTS

2 egg whites
85g (3 oz) caster sugar
250g (9 oz) dark chocolate, broken
  into pieces
300ml (10fl oz) double cream
2 tbsp brandy
6 amaretti biscuits, crushed
icing sugar, to dust
kumquats, to serve (optional)

METHOD

1 Line the cake tin with cling film. Place the egg whites and sugar in a heatproof bowl, place over a pan of simmering water, and whisk for 5 minutes, or until thick, pale, and standing in soft peaks.

2 Melt the chocolate in a bowl over a pan of simmering water. Fold the chocolate into the egg mixture until combined. Whip the cream, then fold it in, along with the brandy. Pour into the prepared cake tin and chill for 4–5 hours, or until set.

3 To serve, turn out on to a plate and remove the cling film. Scatter the amaretti biscuits over the top, then dust with icing sugar and serve with the kumquats, if using.

 serves 8

 prep 20–25 mins, plus chilling

 allow 4–5 hrs for chilling

 20cm (8in) springform cake tin

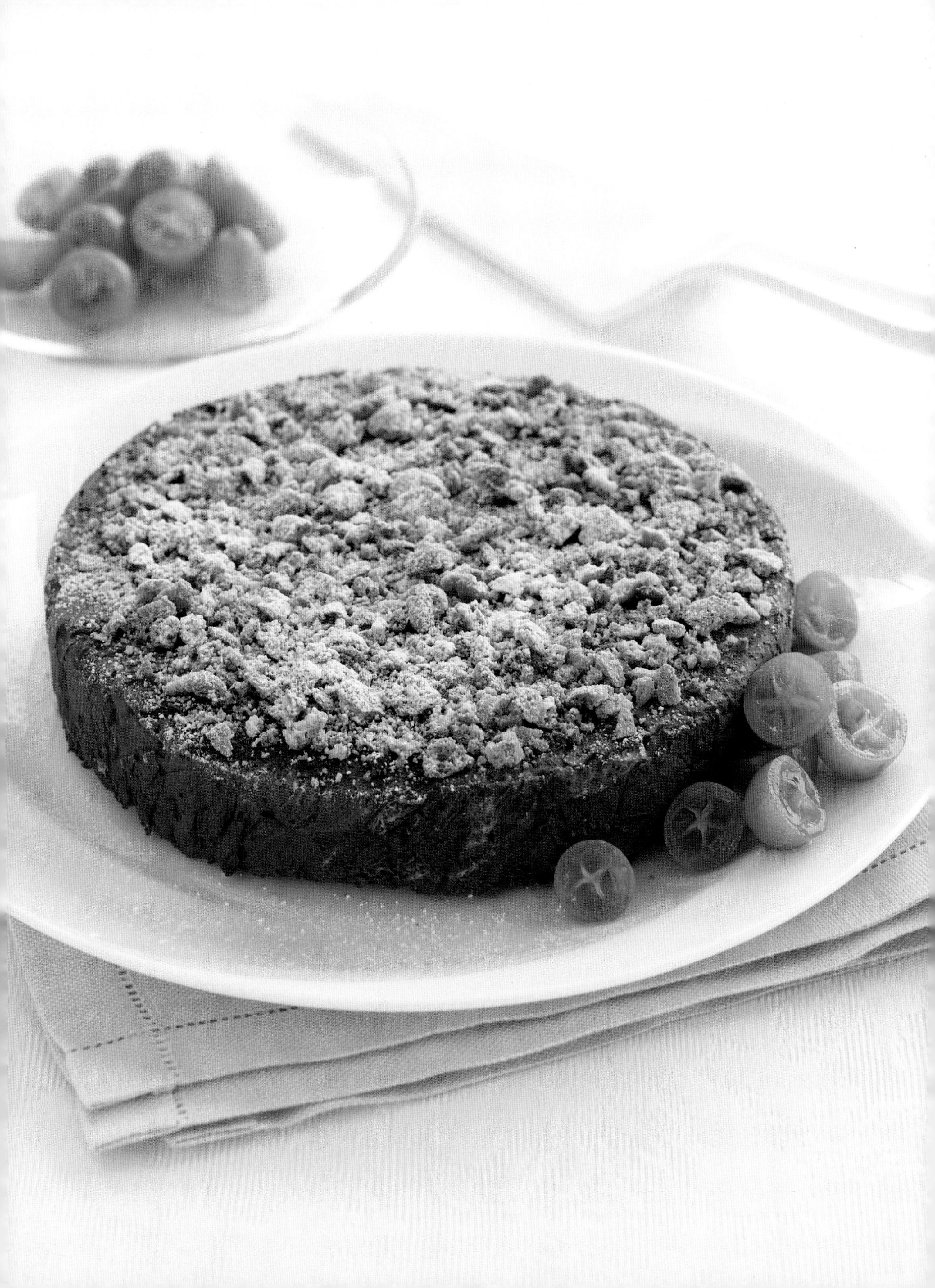

Chocolate almond cake

A dense, moist cake with a rich ganache topping.

INGREDIENTS

plain flour, to dust

115g (4 oz) dark chocolate, broken
  into pieces

115g (4 oz) butter, softened

140g (5 oz) caster sugar

3 eggs, separated

60g (2 oz) ground almonds

30g (1 oz) white breadcrumbs

½ tsp baking powder

1 tsp almond extract

1 tbsp brandy or rum (optional)

For the ganache

115g (4 oz) plain chocolate

60g (2 oz) butter

METHOD

1 Preheat the oven to 180°C (350°F/Gas 4). Grease the tin and line the bottom of the tin
  with greaseproof paper, then dust with plain flour.

2 Place the chocolate pieces in a heatproof bowl over a saucepan of simmering water,
  and melt the chocolate, stirring occasionally. Don't let the bowl touch the water.
  Set aside.

3 Beat the butter and sugar together until pale and creamy. Add the egg yolks one at
  a time, beating well after each addition. Beat in the chocolate. Add the almonds,
  breadcrumbs, baking powder, almond extract, and brandy, if using, and fold in gently
  with a metal spoon.

4 Whisk the egg whites in a large clean bowl until soft peaks form. Fold into the cake
  mixture, then spoon into the tin.

5 Bake for 25 minutes, or until a skewer inserted into the centre comes out clean. Remove
  from the oven and cool on a wire rack.

6 To make the ganache, melt the chocolate and butter together in a bowl over a saucepan
  of simmering water, stirring to combine. Remove from the heat and cool slightly. Using
  a palette knife, spread the ganache over the top of the cake. Allow to set.

serves 6–8

prep 30 mins,
plus cooling
• cook 25 mins

18cm (7in)
loose-bottomed
cake tin

freeze for up to
1 month

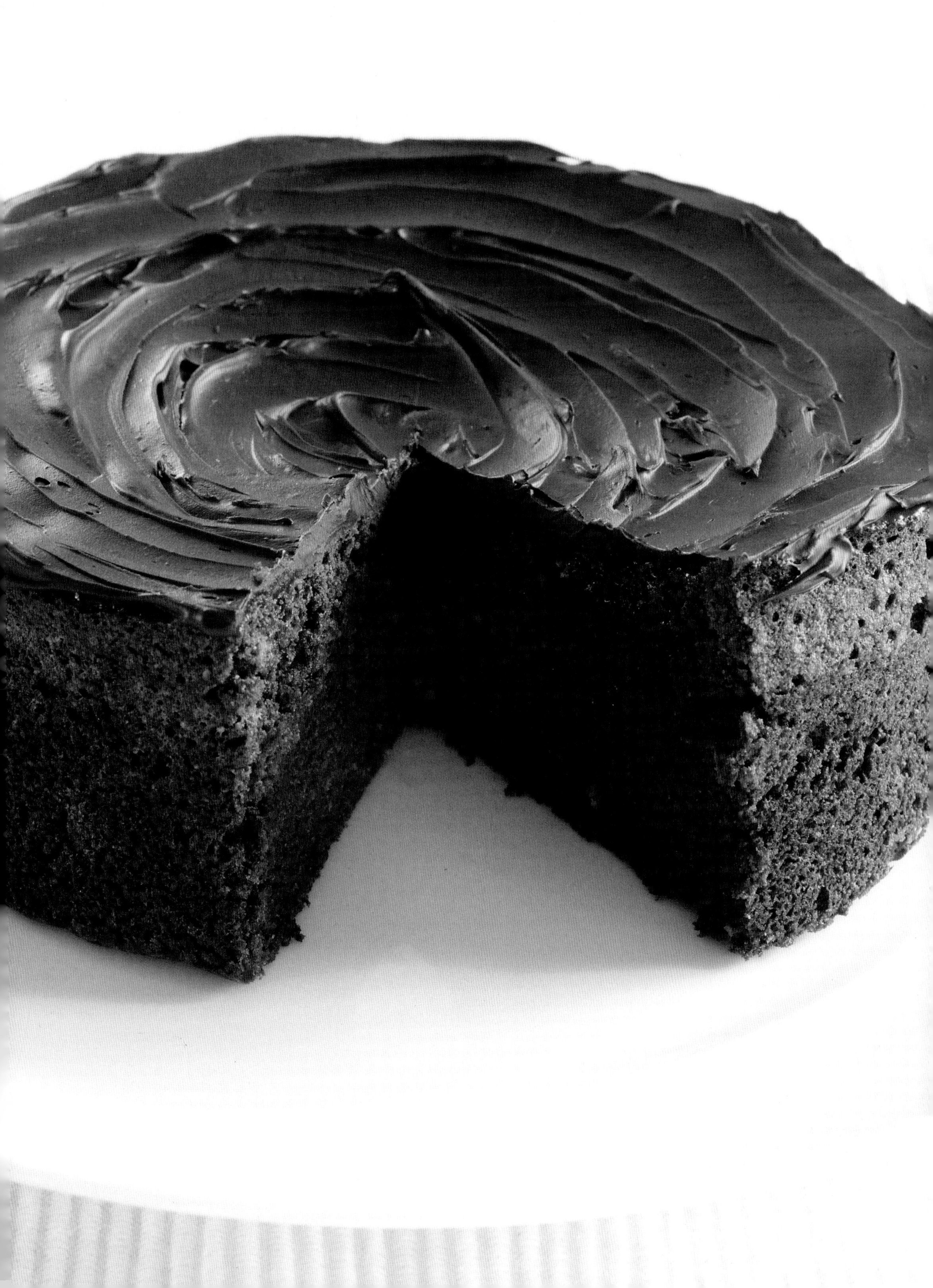

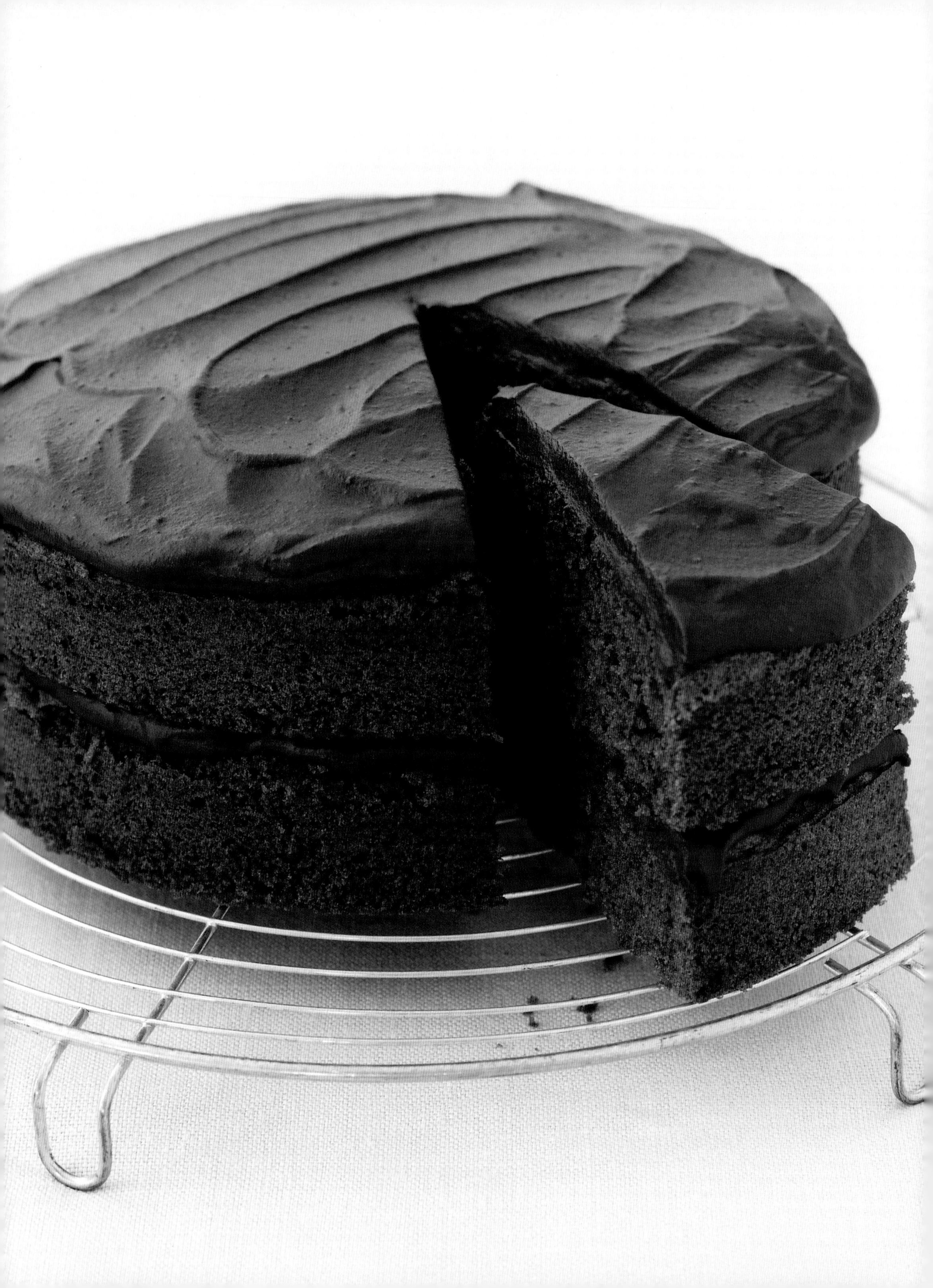

Chocolate cake with chocolate fudge icing

A perennial favourite for birthdays and special treats.

INGREDIENTS

200g (7 oz) self-raising flour
25g (scant 1 oz) cocoa powder
4 large eggs
225g (8 oz) caster sugar
225g (8 oz) unsalted butter, softened
1 tsp pure vanilla extract
1 tsp baking powder

For the chocolate fudge icing

45g (1½ oz) cocoa powder
150g (5½ oz) icing sugar
45g (1½ oz) unsalted butter, melted
3 tbsp milk

METHOD

1 Preheat the oven to 180°C (350°F/Gas 4). Grease 2 sandwich tins, then line with baking parchment. Sift the flour and cocoa powder into a large bowl, and add all the other cake ingredients. Mix together with an electric hand whisk or mixer for a few minutes until well combined. Whisk in 2 tablespoons of warm water from the kettle so the mixture is soft enough to drop easily off the whisk. Divide evenly between the sandwich tins, and smooth the tops.

2 Bake for 35–40 minutes, or until risen and firm to the touch, then leave to cool in the tins for 5 minutes before turning out to cool on wire racks.

3 Meanwhile, make the icing. Sift the cocoa powder and icing sugar into a bowl, add the butter and milk, and mix with an electric hand whisk until smooth and well combined. Add a little extra milk if the mixture is too thick – you need to be able to spread it easily. Spread over the tops of the two cooled cakes, then sandwich them together.

 serves 8–12

 prep 20 mins, plus cooling • cook 40 mins

 2 x 20cm (8in) round sandwich tins • electric hand whisk or mixer

Angel food cake

This American cake uses frosting similar to a meringue.

INGREDIENTS

150g (5½ oz) plain flour
100g (3½ oz) icing sugar
8 egg whites
pinch of cream of tartar
250g (9 oz) caster sugar
few drops of almond extract, or
 vanilla extract
fresh mixed berries, to serve

For the frosting

150g (5½ oz) caster sugar
1 egg white

METHOD

1 Preheat the oven to 180°C (350°F/Gas 4). Sift the flour and icing sugar together into a bowl.

2 Whisk the egg whites and cream of tartar until stiff, then whisk in the caster sugar, 1 tablespoon at a time. Gradually sift the flour mixture over, folding in with a metal spoon. Fold in the almond extract.

3 Spoon the mixture gently into the ring mould and level the surface. Place the mould on a baking tray and bake for 35–45 minutes, or until just firm to the touch.

4 Remove the cake from the oven, and invert the mould on to a wire rack. Leave the cake to cool, then ease out of the mould.

5 To make the frosting, place the caster sugar in a saucepan with 4 tablespoons of water. Heat gently, stirring, until the sugar dissolves. Boil until the syrup reaches soft-boil stage (114–118°C/238–245°F), or until a little of the syrup forms a soft ball when dropped into very cold water.

6 Meanwhile, whisk the egg white until stiff. As soon as the sugar syrup reaches temperature, plunge the base of the pan into cold water to stop the syrup getting any hotter, then pour slowly on to the egg whites, while still whisking, until the frosting holds a stiff peak.

7 Working quickly, because the surface will set quite quickly, spread the frosting over the cake with a palette knife, swirling the surface to give it texture. Serve with mixed berries.

serves 8–12

prep 30 mins,
plus cooling •
cook 35–45 mins

1.7 litre (3 pint)
ring mould • sugar
thermometer

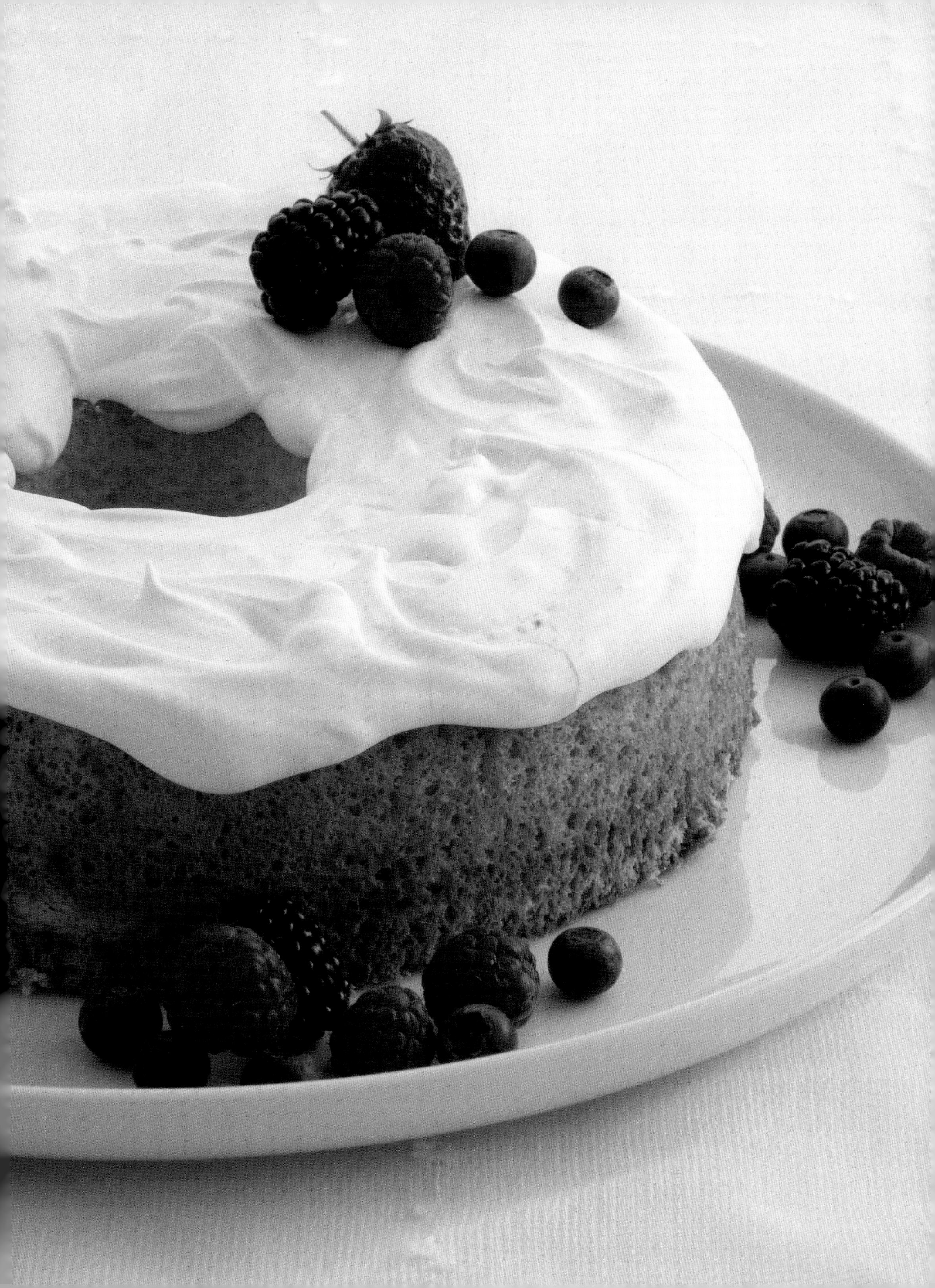

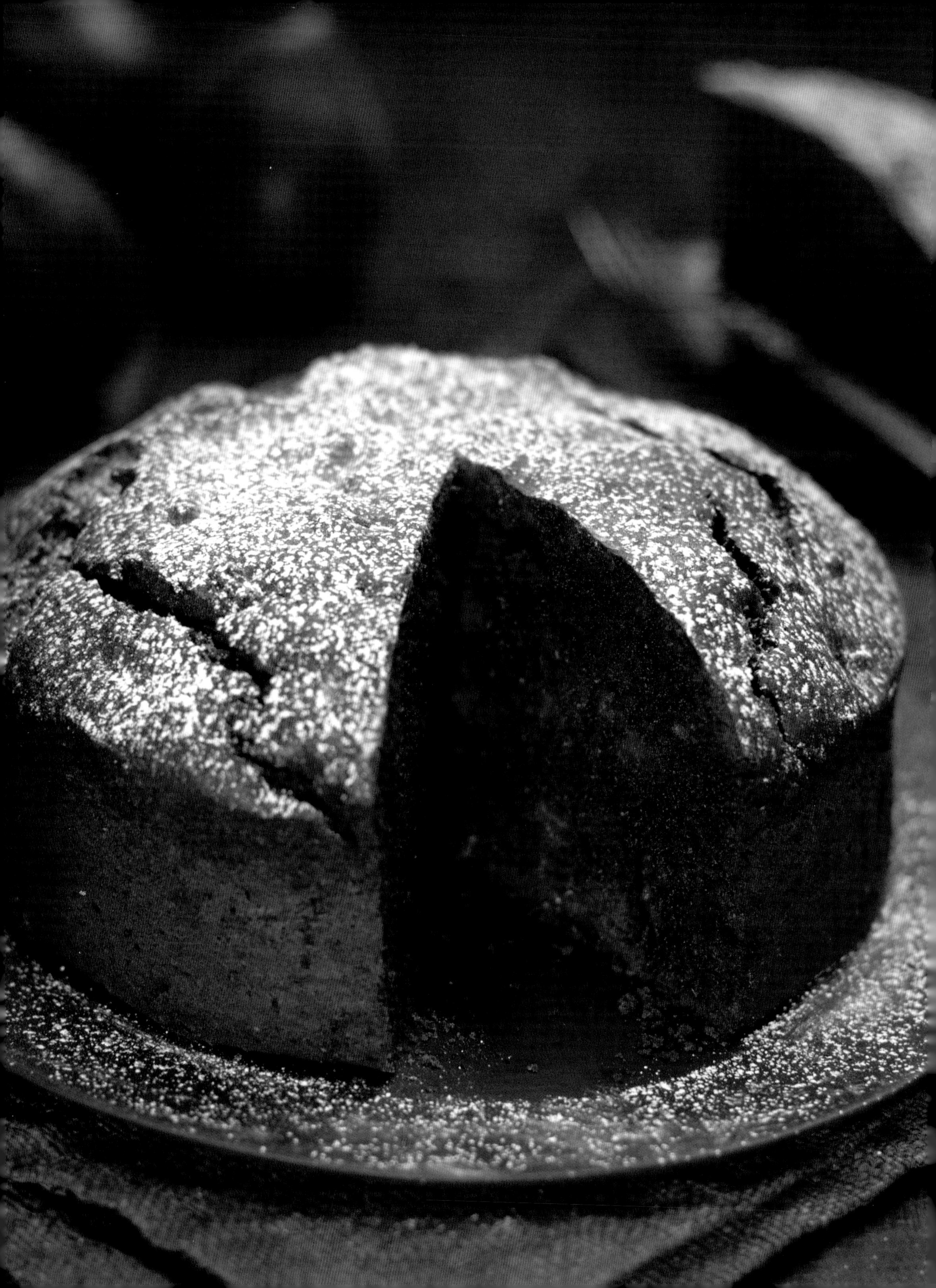

Pear and chocolate cake

This is a gloriously moist, dense cake.

INGREDIENTS

125g (4½ oz) butter, softened, plus extra
  for greasing
175g (6 oz) golden caster sugar
4 large eggs, lightly beaten
250g (9 oz) self-raising wholemeal flour,
  sifted
50g (1¾ oz) cocoa powder
50g (1¾ oz) dark chocolate, chopped
2 pears, peeled, cored, and chopped
150ml (5fl oz) milk
icing sugar, to dust

METHOD

1 Preheat the oven to 180°C/350°F/Gas Mark 4. Line the base of an 18cm (7in)
  springform cake tin with greaseproof paper, and grease the sides with butter.
2 Cream the butter with the sugar until pale and creamy. Beat the eggs in gradually,
  adding a little of the flour each time. Fold in the cocoa powder, chopped chocolate,
  and pears. Add the milk to the mixture and combine.
3 Pour the batter into the prepared cake tin, place it in the oven, and bake for about
  30 minutes, or until firm and springy to the touch. Allow to cool in the tin for
  5 minutes, then remove the tin and transfer the cake to a wire rack to cool
  completely. Dust with icing sugar before serving.

serves 6–8   prep 30 mins,   18cm (7in)
              plus cooling   springform
              • cook 30 mins   cake tin

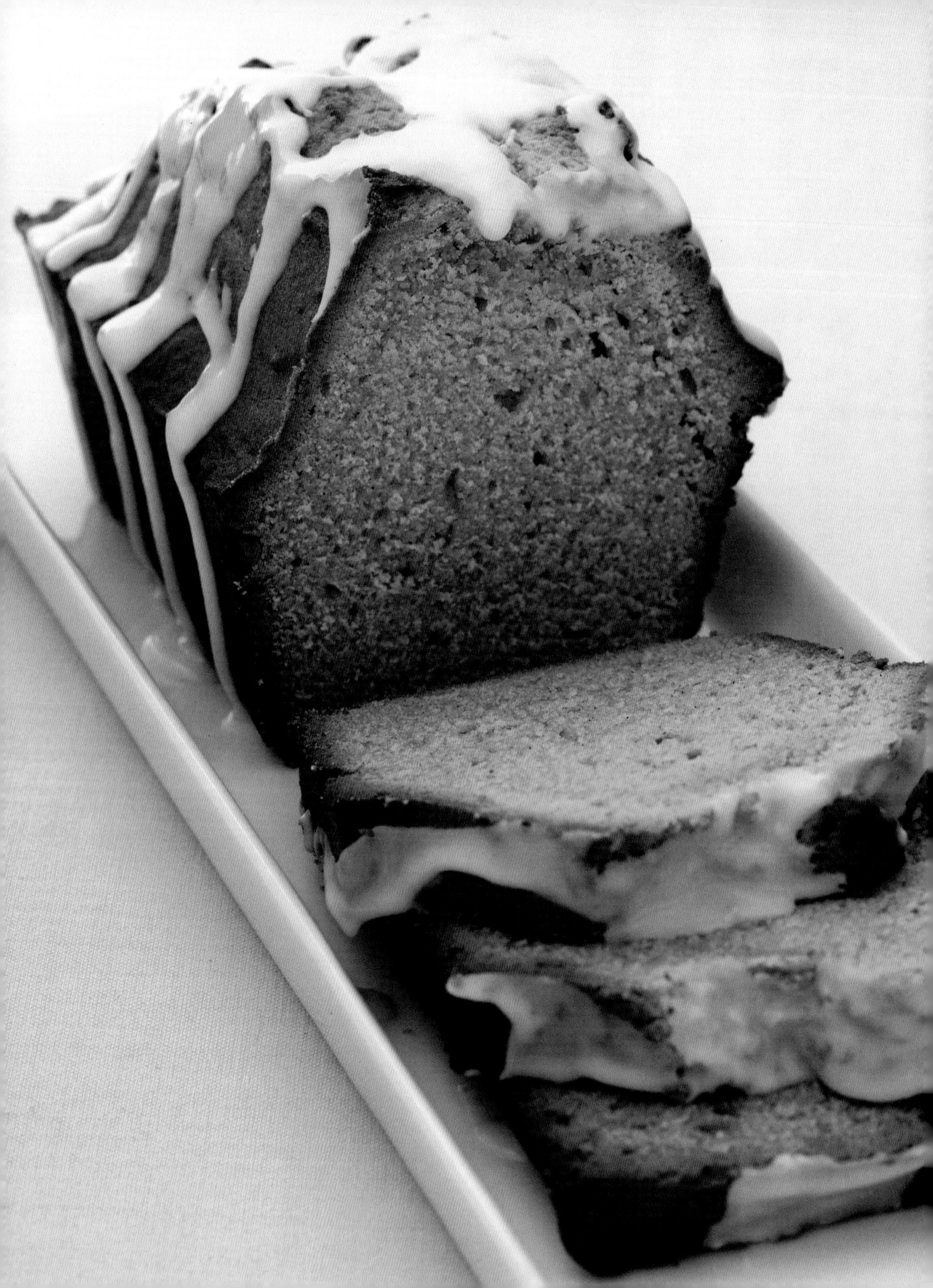

Honey cake

A sweet cake with a delicate taste of honey.

INGREDIENTS

225g (8 oz) butter
115g (4 oz) light muscovado sugar
6 tbsp clear honey
4 eggs, lightly beaten
450g (1lb) plain flour
1½ tsp baking powder
1 tsp ground cinnamon

For the icing

115g (4 oz) icing sugar
1 tbsp clear honey

METHOD

1 Preheat the oven to 180°C (350°F/Gas 4). Grease and line the bottom of the loaf tin.

2 Beat the butter and sugar until they are pale and creamy. Warm the honey in a small pan, then beat into the butter and sugar mixture. Beat in the eggs, a little at a time, beating well after each addition. Add a little flour if the mixture begins to curdle.

3 Sift the flour, baking powder, and cinnamon together, and fold into the cake mixture. Spoon into the prepared loaf tin and level the top. Bake in the centre of the oven for 50–60 minutes. Check after 40 minutes; if the crust is getting too dark, reduce the heat to 160°C (325°F/Gas 3) and cover the crust with a piece of greaseproof paper for the remaining time. The cake is cooked when well risen and if a skewer inserted into the centre comes out clean. Remove from the tin and place on a wire rack to cool completely.

4 Mix the icing sugar with the honey and 1–2 tablespoons of hot water. Spoon the icing over the top of the cake, allowing it to drizzle down the sides.

 serves 10–12

 prep 20 mins, plus cooling • cook 50–60 mins

 900g (2lb) loaf tin

Coconut and lime cake

Layers of tangy lime and coconut sponge and cream cheese icing make this cake an attractive centrepiece.

INGREDIENTS

225g (8 oz) self-raising flour

225g (8 oz) caster sugar

225g (8 oz) unsalted butter, at room temperature

4 large eggs, lightly beaten

50g (1¾ oz) desiccated coconut

grated zest of 1 lime

2 tbsp lime juice

For the icing

100g (3½ oz) icing sugar

grated zest of 1 lime

2 tbsp lime juice

300g (10 oz) cream cheese, at room temperature

15g (½ oz) toasted desiccated coconut, to decorate

METHOD

1 Preheat the oven to 180°C (350°F/Gas 4). Lightly grease the tin and line the base with baking parchment. Sift the flour into a large bowl, add the caster sugar, butter, and eggs and mix with a wooden spoon, electric hand whisk, or mixer until well combined. Mix in the coconut, lime zest, and lime juice. Spoon the batter into the tin and level the top. Bake for 1–1¼ hours, or until risen and firm to the touch. Leave to cool for 5 minutes in the tin, then cool completely on a wire rack. Carefully divide the cake into three equal layers using a serrated knife.

2 To make the icing, sift the icing sugar into a bowl, add the lime zest, lime juice, and cream cheese, and whisk until the mixture starts to thicken. Taste to make sure it is sweet enough. Add more icing sugar if it isn't. Spread over the three layers of the cake, then sandwich them together. Scatter the toasted coconut over the top to decorate.

serves 8

prep 20 mins
• cook 1–1¼ hrs

18cm (7in)
deep round
cake tin

freeze, before
icing, for up to
3 months

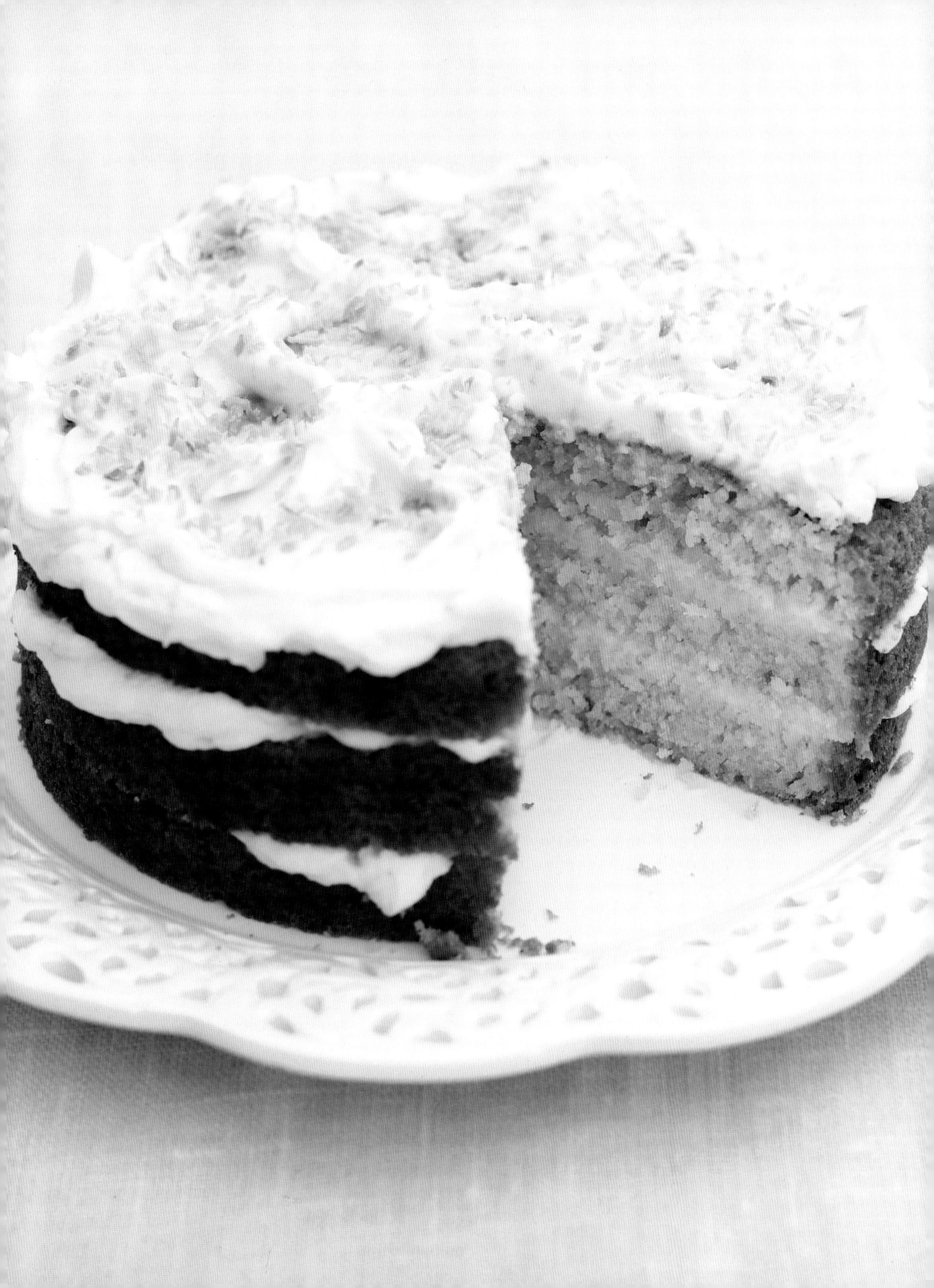

Apple streusel cake

German in origin, streusel is a sweet, sometimes spiced, crumb mixture.

INGREDIENTS

125g (4½ oz) plain flour
125g (4½ oz) butter, at room temperature
125g (4½ oz) caster sugar
1 tsp ground cinnamon
2 large eggs, lightly beaten
½ tsp pure vanilla extract
1 Bramley apple, peeled, cored, and cut into chunks
50g (1¾ oz) sultanas

For the streusel topping

75g (2½ oz) butter, cubed
100g (3½ oz) plain flour
25g (scant 1 oz) ground almonds
50g (1¾ oz) caster sugar or light soft brown sugar
1 tsp ground cinnamon

METHOD

1 Preheat the oven to 180°C (350°F/Gas 4). Lightly grease and line the cake tin with greaseproof paper. Sift the flour into a bowl, add the butter, sugar, cinnamon, eggs, and vanilla extract, and mix with an electric hand whisk until pale, creamy, and well combined. Spoon the mixture into the tin and level the top. Scatter with the apple and sultanas.

2 In another bowl, rub the cubed butter for the topping into the flour with your fingertips until the mixture resembles breadcrumbs. Stir in the ground almonds, sugar, and cinnamon. Scatter over the fruit in the tin and level the top, pressing down slightly. Bake for 1¼ hours, or until a skewer inserted into the cake comes out clean with no trace of uncooked cake mixture (it will probably be a bit damp from the fruit, though). Leave to cool in the tin for 20 minutes and serve warm, or leave to cool completely.

serves 8

prep 20 mins
• cook 1¼ hrs

20cm (8in) round loose-bottomed or springform cake tin
• electric hand whisk

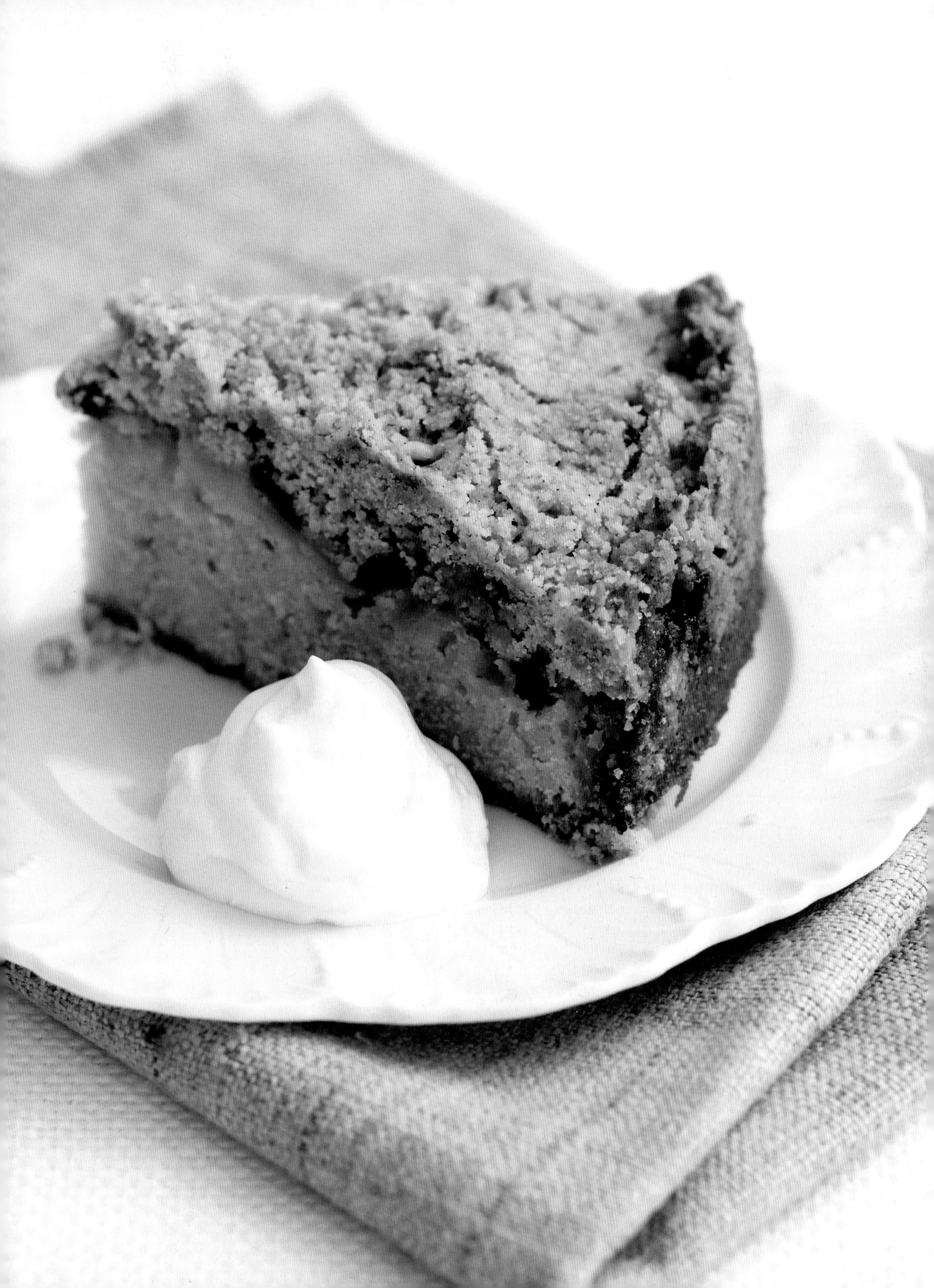

Meringue and rum layer cake

Brown sugar goes well with rum and makes the meringue quite chewy.

INGREDIENTS

85g (3 oz) caster sugar
85g (3 oz) dark soft muscovado sugar
3 egg whites

For the filling

250g (9 oz) mascarpone cheese
30g (1 oz) caster sugar
115g (4 oz) dark chocolate, chopped

150ml (5fl oz) double cream
3 tbsp rum
85g (3 oz) toasted chopped hazelnuts
115g (4 oz) pitted black cherries,
  drained weight
icing sugar, for dusting

METHOD

1 Preheat the oven to 130°C (250°F/Gas ½). Draw 3 x 18cm (7in) diameter circles on a piece of greaseproof paper.

2 To make the meringue, mix the sugars together. Whisk the egg whites until very stiff and gradually whisk in the sugar. Divide among the 3 circles and spread flat. Bake for 1½ hours, or until crisp and dry. Transfer to a wire rack to cool.

3 To make the filling, beat the mascarpone and sugar together in a large bowl. Melt the chocolate in a bowl over a pan of simmering water. Allow to cool for 10 minutes.

4 Stir the chocolate into the mascarpone mixture. Whip the cream until it just holds its shape, then add to the mascarpone, along with the rum, nuts, and cherries.

5 Place a meringue circle on a serving plate, spread half the filling over the meringue, and place a second meringue on top. Spread the remaining chocolate mixture over the second meringue and place the last meringue on top. Chill for at least 30 minutes, then dust with icing sugar before serving.

serves 4–6

prep 30 mins,
plus chilling
• cook 1 hr 30 mins

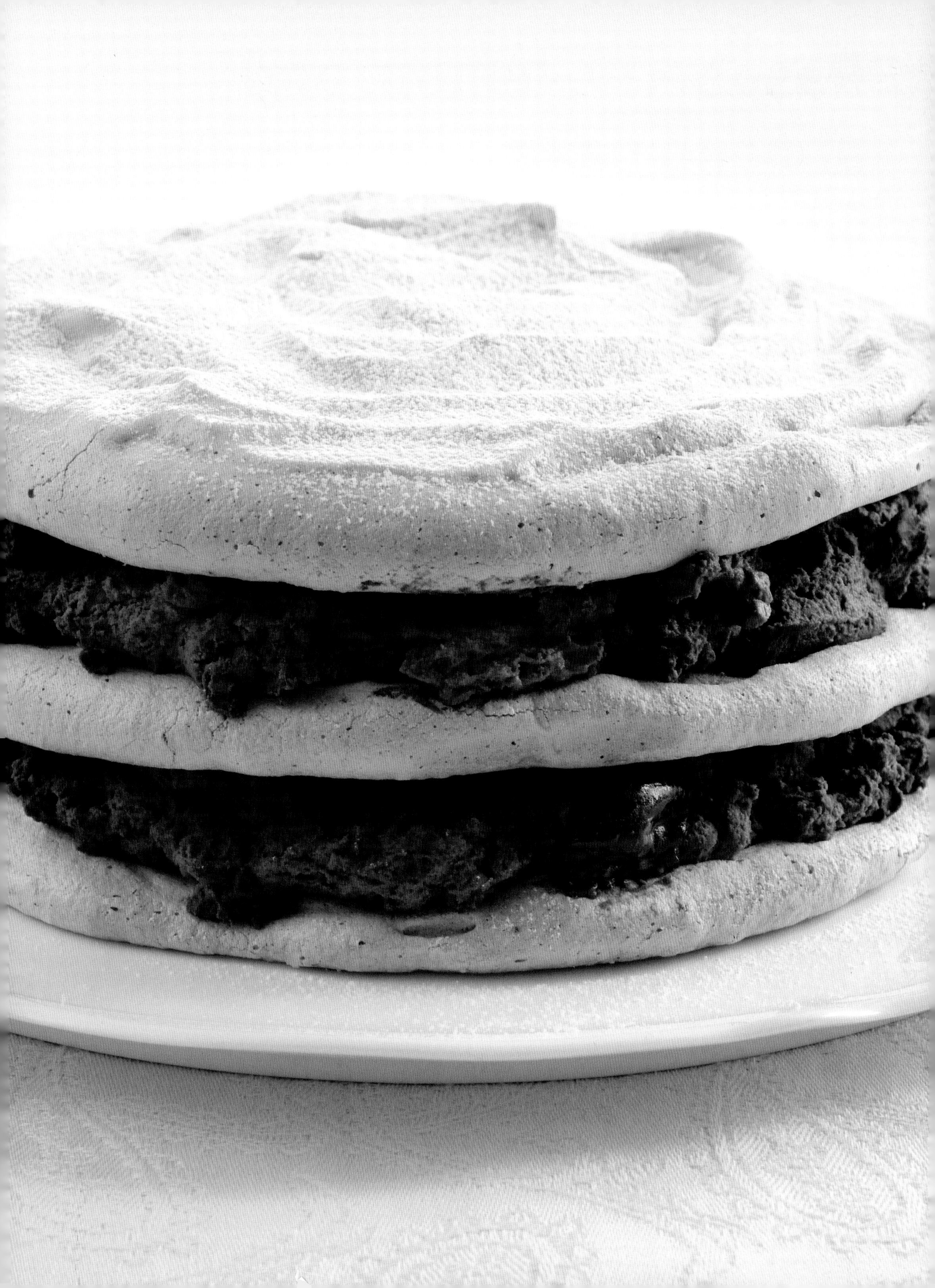

Raspberry, lemon, and almond bake

Sweet almond cake topped with tart raspberries is a moreish treat.

INGREDIENTS

125g (4½ oz) plain flour
1 tsp baking powder
75g (2½ oz) ground almonds
150g (5½ oz) butter, cubed
200g (7 oz) caster sugar
juice of 1 lemon (about 3 tbsp)
1 tsp vanilla extract
2 large eggs
200g (7 oz) fresh raspberries
icing sugar, to dust (optional)

METHOD

1 Preheat the oven to 180°C (350°F/Gas 4). Line the base and sides of the cake tin with baking parchment. Sift the flour into a bowl, add the baking powder and ground almonds, and mix well. In a pan, melt the butter, sugar, and lemon juice together, stirring until well combined.

2 Stir this syrupy mixture into the dry ingredients, then mix in the vanilla extract and the eggs, one at a time, until the mixture is smooth and well combined. Pour into the tin, then scatter the raspberries over the top. Bake for 35–40 minutes, or until golden and a skewer inserted into the cake comes out clean.

3 Cool in the tin for 10 minutes, then turn out and cool completely on a wire rack. Dust with icing sugar before serving (if using). To serve, cut into rectangles.

serves 8

prep 20 mins,
plus cooling
• cook 35–40 mins

20cm (8in) square
loose-bottomed
cake tin

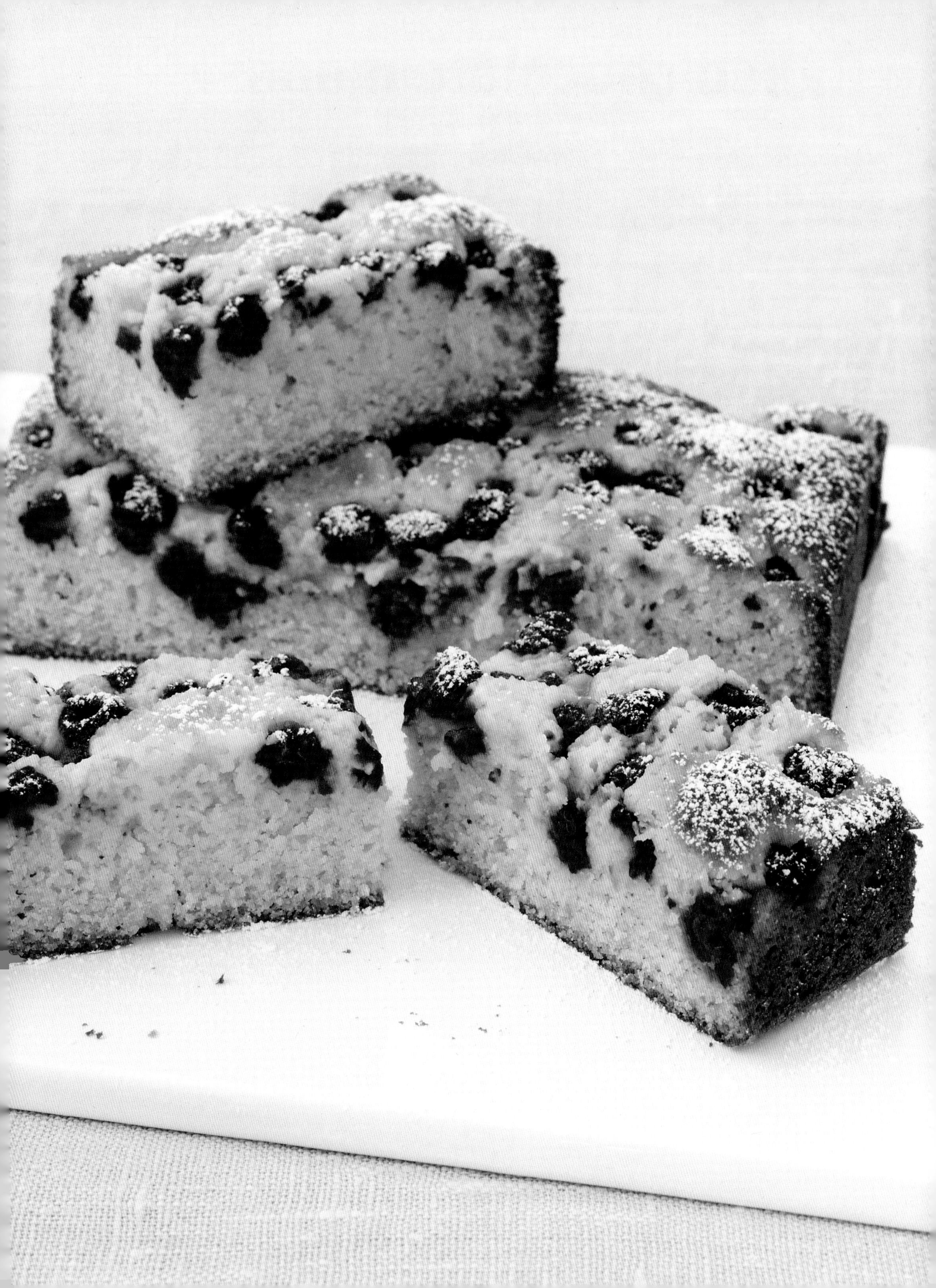

Baked chocolate mousse

This mousse has a cake-like crust and fabulous sticky centre; be careful not to overcook it.

INGREDIENTS

250g (9 oz) unsalted butter, cubed
350g (12 oz) dark chocolate, broken
  into pieces
250g (9 oz) light soft brown sugar
5 large eggs, separated
pinch of salt
cocoa powder or icing sugar, to dust

METHOD

1 Preheat the oven to 180°C (350°F/Gas 4). Line the base of the cake tin with baking parchment. In a heatproof bowl set over a pan of simmering water, melt the butter and chocolate together until smooth and glossy, stirring now and again. Remove from the pan and allow to cool slightly, then stir in the sugar, followed by the egg yolks, one at a time.

2 Put the egg whites in a mixing bowl with a pinch of salt and whisk with an electric hand whisk until soft peaks form. Gradually fold into the chocolate mixture, then pour into the cake tin and smooth the top. Bake for 1 hour, or until the top is firm but the middle still wobbles slightly when you shake the tin. Leave to cool completely in the tin. Remove and dust with cocoa powder or icing sugar before serving. Serve with single cream.

serves 8–12   prep 20 mins,   23cm (9in) loose-
                 plus cooling   bottomed or
                 • cook 1 hr   springform cake tin •
                                     electric hand whisk

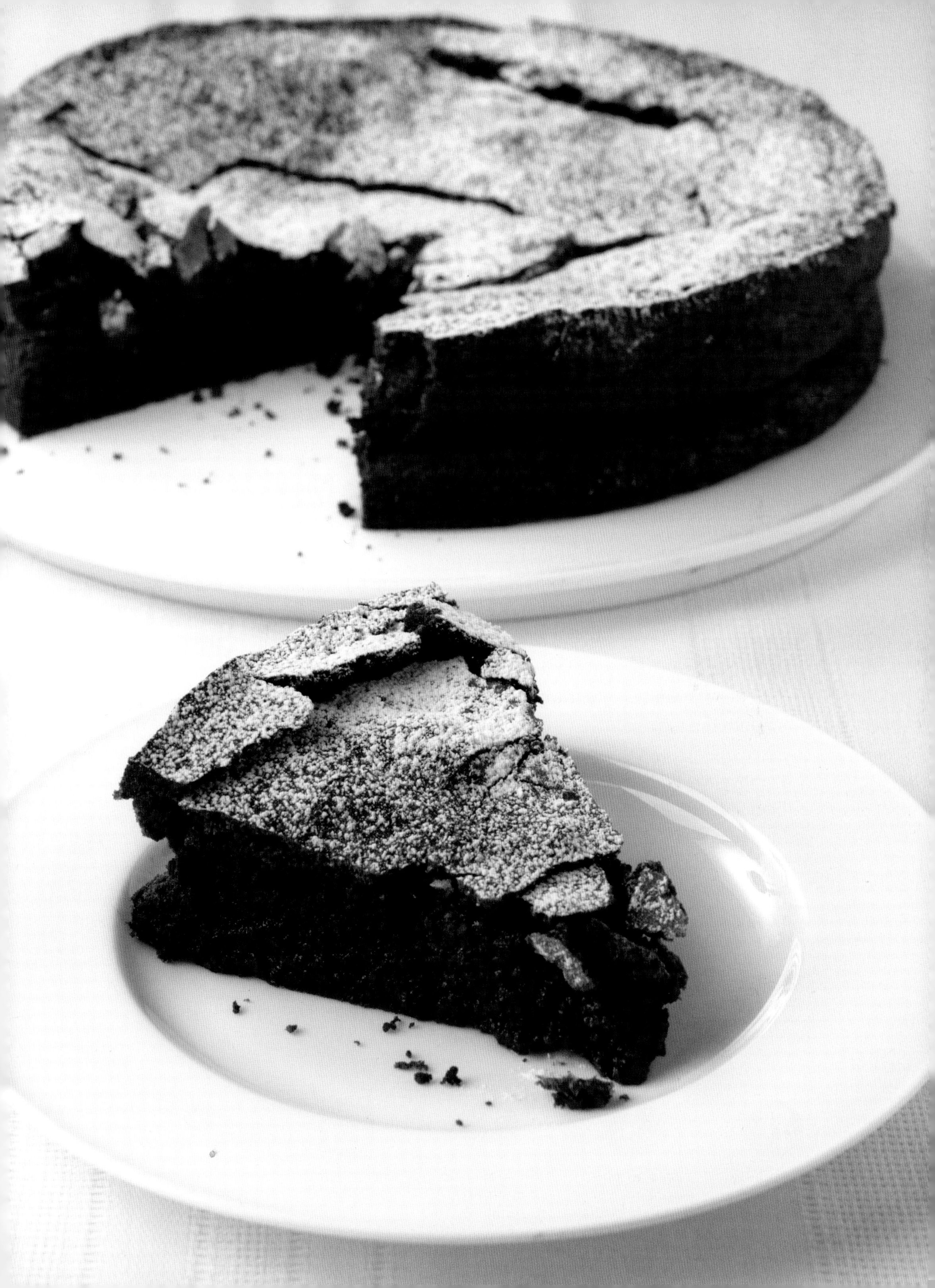

Vanilla cheesecake

This rich yet light cheesecake is guaranteed to be a crowd pleaser.

INGREDIENTS

60g (2 oz) butter
225g (8 oz) digestive biscuits, finely crushed
1 tbsp demerara sugar
675g (1½lb) full-fat cream cheese, at room temperature

4 eggs, separated
200g (7 oz) caster sugar
1 tsp pure vanilla extract
500ml (16fl oz) soured cream
kiwi fruit slices, to garnish

METHOD

1 Preheat the oven to 180°C (350°F/Gas 4). Lightly grease or line the base of the springform tin with greaseproof paper.

2 Melt the butter in a small saucepan over a medium heat. Add the biscuit crumbs and demerara sugar and stir until blended. Press the crumbs over the base of the tin.

3 Combine the cream cheese, egg yolks, 150g (5½ oz) of the caster sugar, and the vanilla in a bowl and beat until blended. In a separate bowl, beat the egg whites until stiff. Fold the egg whites into the cream cheese mixture. Pour the mixture into the tin and smooth the top.

4 Place the tin in the oven and bake for 45 minutes, or until just set in the middle. Remove the tin from the oven and leave it to stand for 10 minutes, or until it sinks back into the tin.

5 Meanwhile, combine the soured cream and remaining sugar in a bowl, and beat until the sugar has dissolved. Pour on top of the cheesecake and smooth the surface. Increase the oven temperature to 240°C (475°F/Gas 9), return the cheesecake to the oven and continue baking for a further 5 minutes. Leave to cool completely on a wire rack, then cover and chill for at least 6 hours. When ready to serve, garnish with slices of kiwi fruit.

serves 10–12

prep 20 mins, plus standing and overnight chilling • cook 55 mins

allow at least 6 hrs for chilling

23cm (9in) springform tin

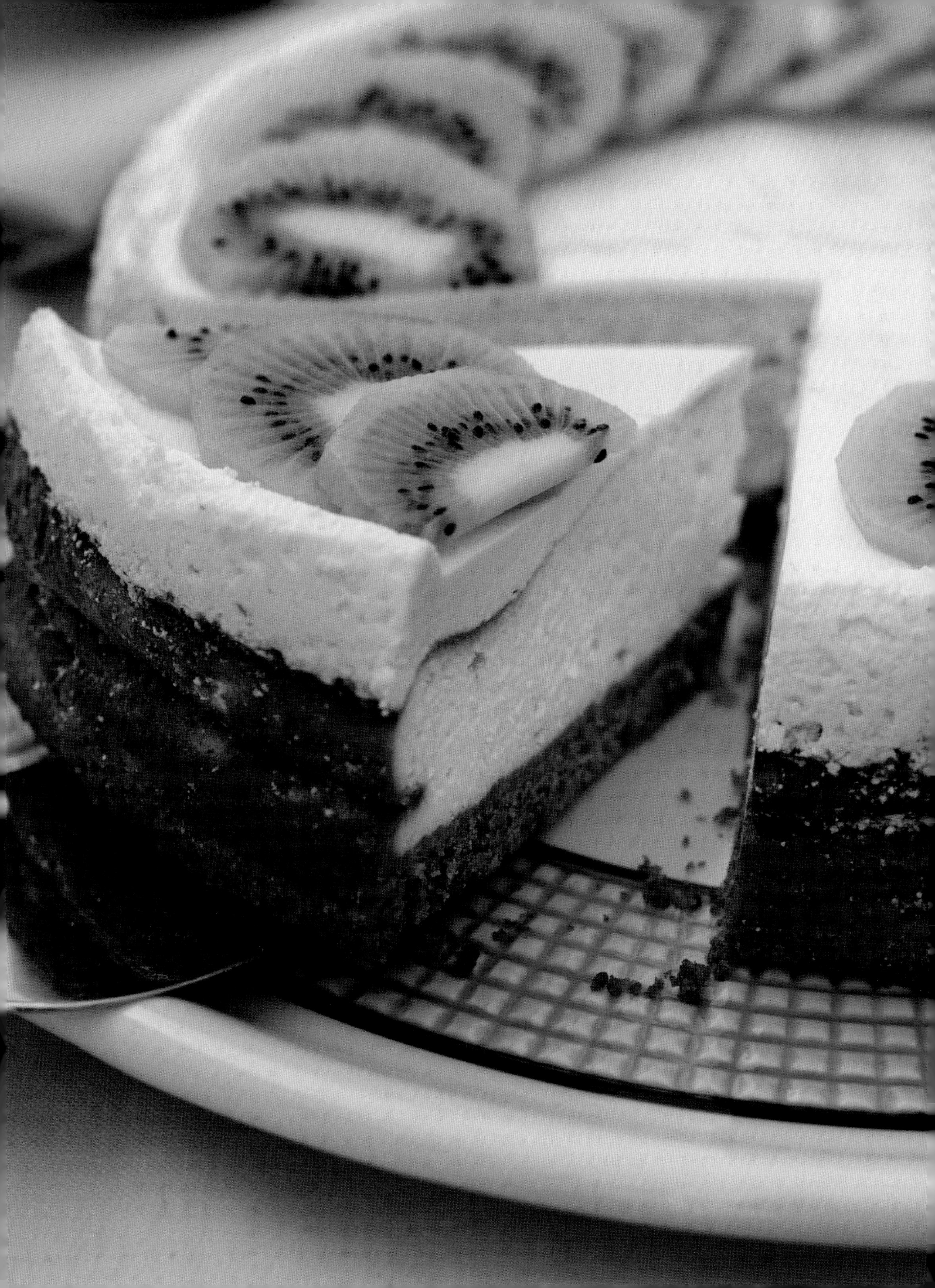

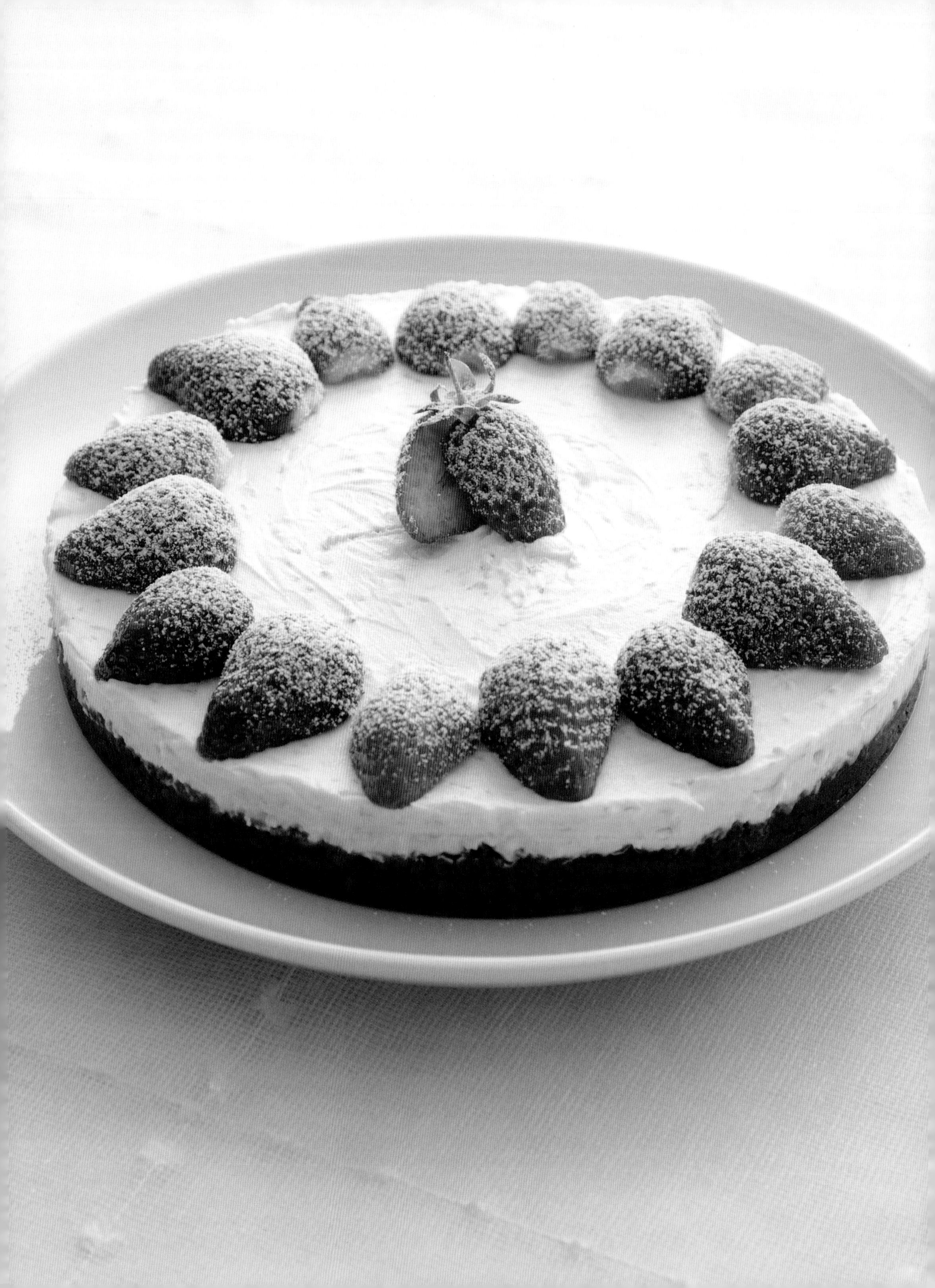

Strawberry cheesecake

This no-cook cheesecake is incredibly easy to make.

INGREDIENTS

50g (1¾ oz) unsalted butter
100g (3½ oz) dark chocolate, broken
  into pieces
150g (5½ oz) digestive biscuits, crushed
400g (14 oz) mascarpone cheese
grated zest and juice of 2 limes
2–3 tbsp icing sugar, plus extra for
  dusting
225g (8 oz) strawberries

METHOD

1 Melt the butter and chocolate in a small saucepan over a very gentle heat, and stir in the biscuit crumbs. Transfer the mixture to the flan tin and press it down firmly and evenly into the tin.
2 Beat the mascarpone in a bowl with the lime zest and juice. Stir in the icing sugar, to taste. Spread the cheese mixture over the biscuit base and refrigerate for at least 1 hour.
3 To serve, hull and halve the strawberries and arrange them over the cheesecake. Dust with icing sugar and cut into slices.

serves 8–10   prep 15 mins,   20cm (8in) round
                     plus chilling   loose-bottomed
                                            flan tin

Rich vanilla buttercream icing

This simple recipe can be used to ice cupcakes and sandwich cake layers together.

INGREDIENTS
115g (4 oz) unsalted butter, at room
   temperature
2 tbsp milk
1 tsp pure vanilla extract
225g (8 oz) icing sugar
food colouring (optional)

METHOD
1 Put the butter, half the milk, and the vanilla extract in a large mixing bowl and beat until smooth and blended using a hand-held electric mixer. Add a few drops of food colouring if you want a more decorative finish.
2 Sift over the icing sugar and, with the mixer on a low speed, continue mixing until the icing is smooth and has a spreading consistency. If it is too stiff, beat in a little extra milk.

makes 350g (12oz)   prep 10 mins   hand-held
                                          electric mixer

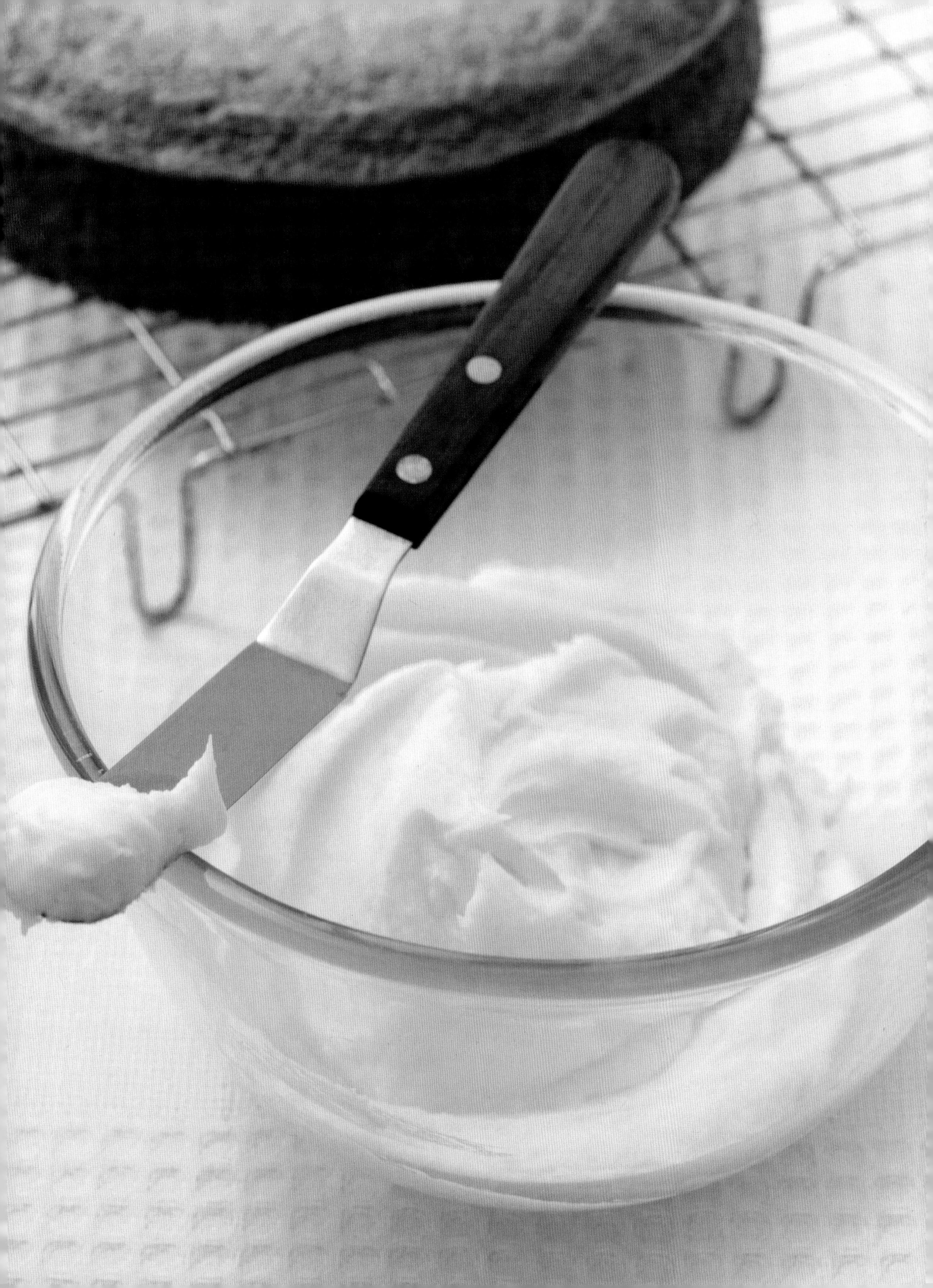

INDEX

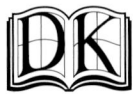

London, New York, Melbourne, Munich, and Delhi

Senior Editor Ros Walford

Editorial Assistant Shashwati Tia Sarkar

Designer Elma Aquino

Jacket Designer Mark Penfound

Senior DTP Designer David McDonald

Production Editor Kavita Varma

Managing Art Editor Richard Czapnik

Indexer Marie Lorimer

DK INDIA

Editorial Consultant Dipali Singh

Designer Neha Ahuja

DTP Designer Tarun Sharma

DTP Coordinator Sunil Sharma

Head of Publishing Aparna Sharma

First published in Great Britain in 2012.
Material in this publication was previously published in Great Britain in *The Cooking Book* (2008), *Cook Express* (2009), *Everyday Easy Cakes & Cupcakes* (2008) and *The Fairtrade Everyday Cookbook* (2008) by
Dorling Kindersley Limited
80 Strand, London WC2R 0RL

Penguin (UK)

10 9 8 7 6 5 4 3 2 1
001–186460–May/12

A CIP catalogue record for this book is available from the British Library.

ISBN 978-1-4093-7497-8

Printed and bound by Hung Hing, China.

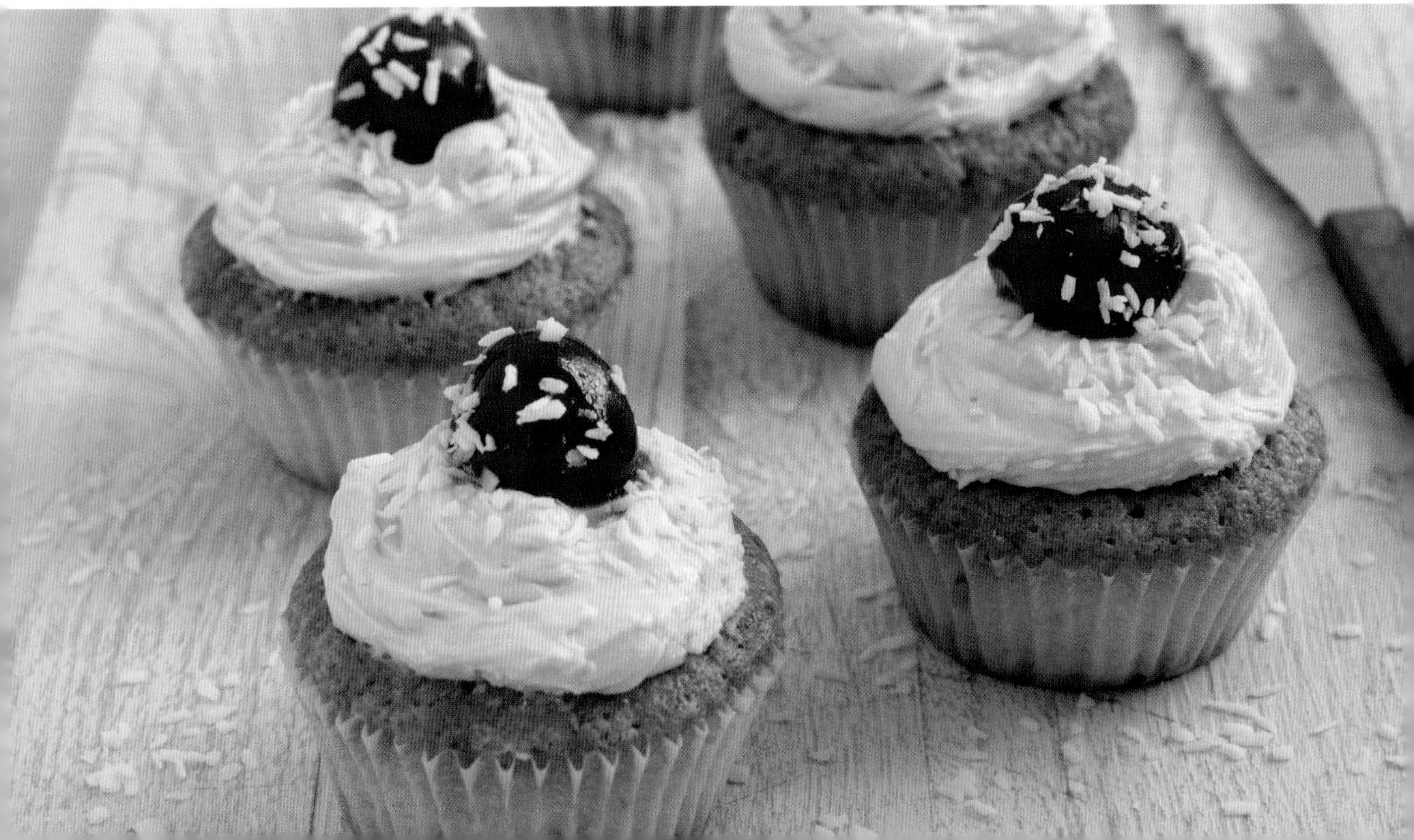